Shubha Vilas, a spiritual see[...]
holds a degree in Engineerin[...]
in Patent Law. In essence, [...]
speaker, lifestyle coach and a storyteller.

He is the author of the bestselling series, *Ramayana: The Game of Life*, that distils thought-provoking life lessons through the gripping narrative of the story of the Ramayana.

His leadership seminars are popular with top-level management in corporate houses. He addresses their crucial needs through enriching discussions and talks.

He periodically interacts with the youth in premier institutes across the world, inspiring them to live a life based on deeper human values. Close to his heart is his role as guide and teacher to school children, helping them learn values through masterful storytelling.

Travelling across the globe and meeting people from all walks of life, he teaches the importance of being governed by dharmic principles, sharing spiritual lifestyle tips and contemporary wisdom to deal with modern-day life situations.

The
Chronicles Of
HANUMAN

Shubha Vilas

Om Books International

Reprinted in 2017 by

Om Books International

Corporate & Editorial Office
A-12, Sector 64, Noida 201 301
Uttar Pradesh, India
Phone: +91 120 477 4100
Email: editorial@ombooks.com
Website: www.ombooksinternational.com

Sales Office
107, Ansari Road, Darya Ganj,
New Delhi 110 002, India
Phone: +91 11 4000 9000
Fax: +91 11 2327 8091
Email: sales@ombooks.com
Website: www.ombooks.com

Text copyright © Shubha Vilas, 2016

ISBN: 978-93-84225-76-6

Printed in India

10 9 8 7 6 5 4 3 2

Contents

Introduction

Whilst the western world is searching for dynamic superheroes who keep getting replaced every few years, the eastern world is happy with a plethora of the already existing ones. The most dynamic amongst them is the evergreen, original superhero—Hanuman—whose stories have entertained and educated civilisations for centuries.

Though Hanuman stories have always been a significant part of Indian culture and ethos, there hasn't been a serious attempt to present them in a contemporary way, without deviating from the original traditional narrative. *The Chronicles of Hanuman* promises to share these stories of Hanuman with the modern world while satisfying the need for entertainment in an innovatively informative way. The aim is to bring together the many tales of Hanuman that have existed in Indian mythology and folklore since thousands of years. With the passage of time, these fascinating tales appeared to fade away from the modern-day readers' consciousness. Hidden within the folds of this book are stories that one would have probably never heard of. The stories which are in philosophical alignment with Valmiki's version of the character of

Hanuman have been included in this book. Others, which aren't, have been carefully avoided to honour the divine personality of Hanuman.

Storytelling is an art of presenting wisdom through jaw-dropping tales. The idea is when the jaw drops, the mouth opens and the wisdom pills are cleverly popped in. The reader doesn't even realise when he has learnt a valuable life lesson!

We learn the formula for achieving success from the story of Hanuman crossing the ocean to find Mother Sita; Hanuman's first interaction with Lord Rama reveals the secrets of communication skills and the Monkey God's ability to find unique solutions to complex problems allows us to learn the power of determination and focus. Hanuman's stories are a source of joy and learning at all levels of life.

Hanuman exemplifies how a true hero has to be a perfect blend of qualities that are paradoxical: strength combined with sweetness, humour flavoured with gravity, sharp intellect complemented with childlike innocence, sensitivity amalgamated with power, traditional wisdom tinged with innovative spirit and fierce determination laced with gentle humility.

The Chronicles of Hanuman is a book that addresses the needs of people across various sections of society. While it is an absorbingly entertaining read for a child; a book that promises to help parents educate their children; a lifestyle management handbook for youth; a motivational guide for those in the competitive world, it also inspires worshippers of Hanuman and is a treasure trove for those who love him.

The author invites you to rediscover your original superhero in an unforgettable manner.

Vedic Tales

The Stolen Pie

A huge monstrous-bodied but saintly-looking personality emerged from the fire. He looked like fire. With reddish hair and a lustrous body, he was impressive to look at. No one in Ayodhya ever thought something like this was possible. They had faith that the King knew what he was doing and the King had equal trust in the sages. The sages had faith in the processes prescribed in the scriptures and the scriptures were always right. Their fiery man was proof enough.

Soon, King Dasharatha held the golden pot of sweet payasam that the fiery man had brought with him. Though it had come out of burning fire, the golden vessel was absolutely cool to touch and so were its contents. King Dasharatha scooped up a portion of the sweet payasam thrice and dropped it into the open palms of his three principle queens. Just as he was about to drop the last portion into the palms of Sumitra, a massive eagle swooped down and snatched a small portion of the payasam and flew away.

Everyone who saw that was bewildered and hoped the incident didn't mean anything inauspicious. One wise sage, who witnessed the mishap, consoled them with his wisdom. He pointed out, 'The eagle that dares to snatch the payasam from such a highly secure assembly cannot be an ordinary bird; it has to be Garuda, the carrier of Lord Vishnu. This is Vishnu Lila in action.'

Meanwhile, the eagle flew off to a distant land where something special was happening. This was the mystical land of Kishkinda in the southern part of the country. On the top of a mountain, in the midst of a dense forest, dressed in the robes of an ascetic was a lady. This was Anjana, the wife of Kesari, the King of the monkey clan. With palms held out in supplication to the Supreme Lord, she was ardently praying for a son who would be the greatest hero the world had seen and the one who would assist humanity in ways unheard of.

The bird opened its claws and, with a splash, the payasam fell into her open palms. At the touch of the payasam, Anjana was jolted to reality. She opened her eyes and found a blob of nectarine-like pie in her palms. Looking up, she saw the divine eagle gazing at her mercifully. There was celestial intervention in her life. Her prayers were answered. She closed her eyes, and offering a prayer of gratitude, swallowed the payasam.

As soon as the payasam entered her body, she could feel a change in herself. She wasn't her normal self anymore. She could instantly feel her womb getting filled. She was pregnant with a force of the gods. All she had to do was prayerfully wait. 'He is coming…'

In the life of the great, accidents happen by higher plan and not by flimsy mistake.

A Divine Birth

Thousands of followers sat around him, waiting for him to open his eyes. None of them knew how long the wait would be. They didn't want to be absent when he did open his eyes. He would go into such a state many times and the experience would be different each time. Not just the duration, but also the way he would come out of the trance. There was always a deep, mysterious secret associated with his waking up. A secret known only to him.

'Rama…Rama…Rama!'

Everyone present there, including his closest associates, were surprised at this sort of an exit he made. Who was Rama? His eyes were still closed. They had a few more moments to admire their hero. Seated in perfect lotus posture, he was the best of the yogis. His brilliantly chiselled body was draped in tiger skin. Three stripes of white ash adorned his forehead, neatly, only to be intercepted at the centre by a vertical third eye that was peacefully closed. His powerful arms were ornamented with armlets of rudraksha beads. His matted hair bunched on top of his head was held in place by a similar string of beads. With a crescent moon on one side and the Ganga flowing from the other, Lord Shiva was a perfect abode of peace and tranquillity.

When he finally opened his eyes, he found his wife, the gorgeous Sati, by his side. Her sixth sense told her that he needed her presence. Seeing her by his side, Lord Shiva lovingly spoke into her ears. He informed her, 'Lord Vishnu is incarnating soon on Earth to annihilate the demonic forces accumulated by Ravana and to put an end to his atrocities. He has instructed all the demigods to take birth as monkeys to assist him in his Lila. I don't want to miss this golden chance to be associated with the incarnation of Lord Rama. I will expand myself to participate in this Rama Lila.'

Sati was extremely saddened to hear this. It seemed to her that she could never really experience the bliss of associating with her husband. When he was with her, he was meditating and when he did come back to consciousness, he was serving. Not wanting to come in the way of her husband's desire to serve Lord Rama, she made a unique request. 'My Lord, if you are planning to expand yourself into a monkey to participate in Rama Lila, may I accompany you in your service by taking the form of your tail?'

Lord Shiva was more than happy to agree to this proposal. But Sati still had one doubt unresolved. She decided to voice it. She was unable to comprehend how Lord Shiva, on the one hand, offered so many boons to Ravana seeming to be his well-wisher and on the other hand, was planning to join the plot to destroy him. Lord Shiva smiled at her innocence and inquisitiveness. He told her that though Ravana had managed to please his ten expansions or rudras, he had dissatisfied and actually angered his 11th expansion. Lord Shiva explained that his 11th expansion would incarnate on Earth as the son of Anjana and would be known as Hanuman.

Satisfied with her husband's intelligence and desire to serve Lord Rama, Sati embraced Lord Shiva. Soon, both of them transformed into monkeys and began enjoying conjugal pleasures. Their union converged into an energetic conception that Lord Shiva handed over to Vayu (the Wind God), for delivering it at the appropriate time to Anjana. The Wind God was unsure of his ability to handle the power bestowed on him for long. The conception of Lord Shiva was so hot that if it were to be in his possession, the searing winds would continue blowing and the world would eventually perish. He invoked the presence of the Sapta Rishis (Seven Sages) and requested them to handle the conception of Lord Shiva till the appropriate time arrived. These Seven Sages brought a metal leaf from the Mandakini Ganga and placed the powerful energy in it and assured the Wind God of its safety in their custody till he came to reclaim it.

Meanwhile, in the heavenly planets, Brihaspati, the guru of the demigods had cursed one of his servants whose name was Punjikasthali to become a monkey in the earthly realm. As a result, she was reborn on Earth as Anjana. When she attained youth, she married a Vanara King named Kesari. Despite long years of their marriage, they were unable to have a child. Anjana decided to perform austerities to invoke the blessings of the Lord. As she was absorbed in tapasya (austerity), the Wind God, who was keenly observing her realised that she was purified enough to receive the grace of Lord Shiva.

Suddenly, Anjana felt an invisible force taking hold of her. She panicked and began to scream. She yelled so that she would curse the one who was responsible for this. That was when the Wind God appeared in front of her and explained that he was here under the direction of Lord Shiva to offer her the child that would be the greatest hero the world had ever seen. He would be a direct expansion of Lord Shiva and the son of the Wind God. Hearing this, Anjana gracefully accepted the powerful conception.

While his wife was engaged in tapasya to beget a son, Kesari decided to perform a different type of austerity to please Lord Shiva. He wandered around various sites of pilgrimage offering ardent prayers. As he was travelling from one holy place to another, he reached Gokarna. At this place, he found a monster named Shaambasaadhana torturing innocent sages. He challenged this demon and after a gruesome fight, he managed to slay him by hitting him forcefully on his chest.

Pleased with Kesari for relieving them of their burden, the sages collectively blessed him—he would have a powerful son who would become the protector of the innocent and destroyer of evil in this world. To make this happen, they offered him a Shiva mantra. As soon as Kesari chanted this mantra, Lord Shiva appeared before him and blessed him. Instantly, Kesari felt himself empowered with Shiva Shakti. He returned home in time to see his wife Anjana back from her mission.

On seeing each other, the couple embraced joyfully. Shiva Shakti that resided within Kesari was now transmitted to Anjana and Kesari became his normal self. In due course, the world's greatest superhero would be born.

Selflessness gives birth to heroism.

An Attempt to Abort

A King entered stealthily into another King's palace in the dead of the night. This was not a regular occurrence. But when it did happen, it meant something was going to go wrong. This was such a crucial task that he didn't want to risk appointing anyone else.

As he was walking down the secret tunnel below the palace, Bali, the King of a section of the Vanara clan was thinking of all the events that led up to this bold and rather risky decision.

It all began when Narada, the transcendental spaceman descended upon the lanes of Kishkinda. People were awestruck by his charisma. He was effulgent and extremely handsome. Singing in his divinely melodious voice and playing the chords of his famous Veena, he danced his way towards the palace of the King. King Bali greeted Narada respectfully, knowing full well that he had a message to convey. If he had chosen to come all the way, the message had to be of utmost importance to Bali.

After impatiently going through the formalities of reception, Bali sat next to Narada to hear what he had to say. Finally, Narada revealed the secret. A secret that shook

Bali to the core and, in an instant, converted him from a confident King to an insecure monkey. In the womb of Anjana, the wife of King Kesari, an expansion of Lord Shiva was to be born. Rumours were rife in the heavenly realms that this child would be the greatest hero on Earth and his strength would surpass Bali's by thousand folds. Initially, Bali panicked but later, as he thought deeply, he realised that any danger, if evaded, wasn't a danger at all. He had to only act intelligently.

Here he was walking into the palace of Kesari in the dead of the night. Using his negotiation skills, he had gained access to the royal kitchen. There, someone was waiting for him. She was the personal cook of the pregnant queen. She had been appointed by Kesari to cater to the diet restrictions of the pregnant royal queen. This lady seemed to be an expert at catering to the diet needs of pregnant ladies. However, now, she was going to be served something else. A special dish that Bali had got.

The next morning, she carefully heated up the liquid Bali had given her the previous night. She could sniff some metal content in it. It had been expertly made, so no one could make out what it really was. All Bali had told her was that this potion would do its job. But, she wasn't just another person, she knew exactly what the potion had. As she carried a glass containing the piping hot liquid, her hands shook slightly. She knew it was wrong. It was terribly wrong to feed a heavily pregnant woman a drink comprising five metals: gold, copper, iron, tin and zinc. One of these could not just kill the child, but also, the mother.

She closed her eyes as she saw Anjana gulp down what the latter had been told was a health drink that revitalises the mother and the baby in the womb. As she took back the glass from the queen, she keenly observed her face for any reaction. Surprisingly, there was none. She waited for a full minute, just in case it took that long to see the effect. Nothing! Not knowing what to do, she just walked back to the kitchen. That day, she kept walking back and forth between her kitchen duties and attending to the queen, desperately waiting to see some change. Nothing ever happened to the queen.

The next day, Queen Anjana was taken to the labour room. Her contractions had started. Expecting the news of miscarriage, the Bali's aide stood right outside the delivery room. Instead, she was greeted with the cry of a newborn. While everyone celebrated, she sank to her knees. How could a child be born after the mother had drunk the amalgam of those five deadly metals? Gathering herself after some time, she ran into the room to see the child who had been miraculously saved from death. When she saw the child's face, she fainted.

The monkey baby was smiling at her and was born with earrings made of an alloy of those five metals. Instead of destroying him, these had ended up adorning him.

Insecurity distorts the beauty of the soul, while innocence decorates one's character.

When Hanuman Swallowed the Sun

For the first time in the history of the heavens, there was a power cut. Absolute darkness prevailed in the heavenly realms. There was utter chaos everywhere. How could there be darkness in a place that is illuminated by the sun? The power cut happened while Indra's most important conference of the year was underway. The celestial administrative heads had all come together to report their activities.

Everybody seemed clueless about the power cut. As far as they knew, nothing ever went wrong with the systems in the heavens. A guard came stumbling into the room, which by then was partially illuminated by the fire of Agni. 'O powerful gods, I have bad news for you all. A monkey child has swallowed the sun, mistaking it to be a big red fruit.'

'WHAT!' Every demigod in that room was completely aghast. Who can ever swallow the sun?

The guard continued, 'Not just that, since it was the time of the eclipse, Rahu had come to swallow the sun at the same time. But when he saw that the baby monkey had already swallowed the sun, he tried to argue with the baby monkey about his rights. The baby monkey took Rahu to be another big fruit and caught him too. There is complete confusion and shock in the heavenly realms now. Kindly do something to bring things under control.'

After listening to this horrific tale, Indra instantly mounted his elephant carrier, Airavata, to reach the scene of disaster. Not wanting to delay the release of the sun from the mouth of the monkey, he threw his Vajra (thunderbolt weapon) with the help of sabdha bedhi (sonic weaponry) which enabled him to strike his target by focussing on the sound emitted by it. But, interestingly, the elephant was so eager to fight, that even before Vajra reached the monkey, Airavata came in the way. As soon as the baby monkey saw the huge white elephant, he rushed towards him and wanted to shove him also into his mouth. Indra panicked when he saw the baby zooming towards him like a comet. That's when the Indra's Vajra hit the baby monkey square in the chin. No extraordinary human or even demigod could have survived such a blow. The jawbone cracked and the baby monkey became unconscious. As he fell, his mouth opened and the sun and Rahu rushed out of it.

The demigods were relieved that the sun had been restored to the original position. But they had a presentiment of something more disastrous. Before attacking the baby monkey, none of them had even considered seeking an opinion from Lord Brahma or Brihaspati. The baby monkey had fallen with a thud into a cave in the Earth. He was completely unconscious and practically lifeless.

Suddenly, another catastrophe struck. The air-circulation system stopped. None of them were able to breathe. 'What's happening in the heavens today?' There was utter confusion once again. This time, though, they decided to consult Lord Brahma for his practical wisdom. Lord Brahma was their supreme guide; he always analysed a situation from a broader perspective instead of relying on immediate needs and short-term results. He explained to the gods, 'This baby monkey is none other than the son of Vayu, and was named Anjaneya (son of Anjana). This baby monkey is, in fact, an expansion of Lord Shiva. He shall play a pivotal role in the destruction of Ravana. Since his son is hurt, the Wind God has protested by withdrawing all air from the universe. His personal suffering has led to universal suffering.' Lord Brahma urged all the demigods to accompany him in reviving the child and making the Wind God happy.

The atmosphere in the cave was tense. An aggrieved father was gazing at his lifeless son, teary-eyed. Lord Brahma walked up to the monkey child and sprinkled a few drops of holy water from his kamandalu (water pot) and rubbed his hands over the child's body. Within moments, the child sat up looking at all the divine personalities standing around him. Seeing the broken jaw of the baby monkey, Lord Brahma declared, 'This day on, this child will be known as Hanuman ("Hanu" means jaw), reminding the world of this wonderful feat in his childhood. Since he is the Wind God's son, he will be known as Marut-suta or Maruti. His body is now solid like Indra's Vajra, and this shall give him another name, he would be called Bajrangi. I also grant him the boon that he will live as long as I live. No one will ever be able to kill or even defeat him. He will not be bound by the laws of nature.'

Lord Brahma implored all the demigods to bestow their choicest blessings on this wonder child. Each one came forward and blessed the child. Agni gave him the boon that fire would never affect him. Indra blessed him with the boon that he would be as famous as himself and no weapon would be able to injure him. Brihaspati bestowed upon him the knowledge of Ayurveda and all the fruits, plants and trees in the world. The Sun God offered to teach him all the Vedas at an appropriate time. Dhanvantari provided him the healing touch. Vishwakarma, the Celestial Architect, gifted him unbelievable intelligence, clarity of thought and creativity. His father, Vayu, blessed him with the power of speed.

Once all the demigods had offered their boons, Lord Brahma came forward and placed a diamond necklace around Hanuman's neck. He said, 'Now, I will give you the highest benediction you can get, my child. You will be the eternal servant of the Lord. This diamond necklace that I placed around your neck will remain invisible to the eyes of the world. The one who recognises this necklace will be your eternal Lord and master. The moment you meet your master, every bone in your body will melt.'

When all these boons were being bestowed, Hanuman looked serious. As soon as Lord Brahma declared him to be the eternal servitor of the Lord, Hanuman began to beam.

When everyone left, only one thought ruled Hanuman's head. If this was the kind of attention he was going to receive after such a small mischief, it was worth trying more…

When innocence is labelled a mistake, then, punishment will be labelled injustice.

Most times, counting blessings is more difficult than counting pain, since blessings have to be counted geometrically and pain arithmetically.

A Monkey's Restlessness

His father couldn't believe what he saw that day. He wasn't running. He wasn't jumping. He wasn't skidding. He was walking. Hanuman was walking that day.

As soon as he saw his son walk back home that day, Kesari had a doubt in his mind. He was expecting something to happen sooner or later. Hanuman was taking the sages too casually. His fears were confirmed when he saw Hanuman's downtrodden face. He was not just sad, but was deeply contemplative. Till that day, Kesari had never seen his son in deep thought. He was a man of action, or rather, a monkey in action.

He walked up to his son and kneeled down. Holding his face lovingly, he asked, 'What happened, my son?' Hanuman's reply left him speechless. He said, 'I want to study.'

Kesari couldn't understand the genesis of this idea. He was bewildered and decided to investigate the matter himself. He knew that Hanuman wouldn't be able to convey everything that had happened. There was a higher power at work that day.

Sitting with a bunch of very senior sages, Kesari heard everything they had to say about his son. Initially, everything they said was disturbing, but, the conclusion was encouraging.

Every day, Hanuman would be at the riverbank looking out for new ways of harassing people. The sages, hardened by austerities, were his soft targets. While most people stayed away from these sages fearing their supernatural powers, Hanuman felt naturally attracted to them. Of course, there was nothing constructive he offered them or gained from them. He did all this for fun. He would constantly look for some activity to occupy his restless, wild mind.

When the sages bathed, Hanuman would make big holes in their clothes. He would break their kamandalus by hitting them against a tree trunk. He would then wait for them to come out and watch their disturbed faces and derive sadistic pleasure. If they would take longer to come out, he would enter the waters and pull their legs from underneath. The sages would panic thinking it to be a water-crocodile attacking. Sometimes, if he saw them standing next to the riverbank and offering prayers to the sun with closed eyes, he would jump onto their shoulders and pull their long beards. His favourite trouble-game would take place after the sages would come out of the river freshly bathed. He would be waiting for them patiently. He would quickly fill up his mouth with water and spit at them like a water sprout. Being thus contaminated, the sages would be forced to have a bath again. This loop would be repeated several times with a single sage, sometimes for hours together.

Finally, fed up of being harassed by this maniac regularly at the riverbank, the sages decided to abandon their regular water source and each of them found different water sources to have their baths. After several days of drought in his fun, Hanuman understood what the sages were up to. He decided to venture into their hermitages for his daily quota of fun and entertainment.

One day, the sages were engaged in a serious discussion on the import of the scriptures when Hanuman entered their ashram. He was seated on a tree a little away from where the meeting was happening. Suddenly, his eyes fell on a bunch of succulent fruits that were hanging on the tree under which these sages were seated. He jumped and as soon as he landed, the branch on which he landed broke off. He, somehow, managed to jump off at the nick of time and land on another branch, which also broke off. Again, he managed to save himself from the fall. But he couldn't prevent the two broken branches from crashing right into the assembly of sages. Though no one was hurt, the sages were furious with this mischief-monger.

But there was one incident that crossed the respected sages' threshold of tolerance. Earlier than usual, one morning, much before sunrise, Hanuman had ventured into the forest in search of enjoyment. He chanced upon a tiger fighting with an elephant. He walked up to them, and, to their shock, held the elephant by its tusks, pulling it away from the tiger. He then held the tiger by its tail with his other hand and began to drag both the helplessly stunned beasts. After dragging them to quite a distance, he tied them up to two poles on both sides of the door of an ascetic's hermitage. This done, Hanuman hid himself to watch the fun.

Soon, the ascetic named Trinabindu, opened his door carrying a water-pot in his hand, eager to attempt answering nature's call in the morning. When he stepped out, his eyes were fixed on the door. Since the sun hadn't yet risen, it was still quite dark. But, he was used to this routine and knew how to navigate his way through the darkness. As he stepped out of the doorway into the porch, he got the scare of his life on seeing a tiger standing right at the entrance, roaring at him. He shrieked, dropping his water-pot and ran back into the house and locked the door. He usually suffered from constipation, but today's incident had frightened him such that he urgently felt the need to release. Gathering courage, for he knew the tiger was tied to a pole, he decided to step as far away from the tiger as possible and attempt an exit. This time, when he walked out, he shrank away from the tiger. Just when he was about to step out, he was confronted by a wild elephant. He screamed again and ran indoors.

By this time, Trinabindu was writhing in agony. There was turmoil inside his body and a catastrophe outside his house. He had no idea who had played this wild prank. He was boiling with rage when he heard peals of laughter coming from close by. He ran up to his window and saw Hanuman rolling on the ground, holding his tummy and laughing.

In great anger and with the desire to prevent the restless monkey from offending other revered sages, Trinabindu picked up his kamandalu and flicking water from inside, hurled it towards Hanuman, pronouncing a curse. He cursed, 'You impudent child, your power and speed have made you very proud. Since there is no one who knows how to utilise this power and speed, you are misusing it and causing harm to others. I curse you that you would forget all you powers until and unless reminded about them by someone.'

As soon as the curse was pronounced, Hanuman became quiet. He began to look around unable to comprehend how he had reached the forest and what he was doing there lying on the ground. He began to contemplate what the purpose of his life was and how he should spend his time productively.

As he walked back to his father, Kesari's palace, an intense desire took firm shape in his heart. The desire to acquire knowledge...

Hidden within every act of naughtiness is a seed of intelligence. When waters of inspiration and encouragement nourish this seed, flowers of responsibility and fruits of dynamic contribution will blossom.

An Inter universal Flying School

His second flight to the sun was a more sober one. Things had changed from his last adventure. The previous journey was born out of blissful ignorance and this time, the thirst for knowledge was the driving force. He had gone to challenge the last time, he wished to submit this time. What was once a conquest was now an act of seeking forgiveness.

Surya (the Sun God), panicked seeing him again. He still remembered the trauma of being swallowed up and rendered helpless for several hours. The unpleasant memory was still fresh in his mind. Who would forget humiliation, especially, if it happened just once in one's entire lifetime? But when he looked carefully, he saw that the boy was standing with his hands folded in supplication. The Sun God was surprised.

In a voice filled with genuine humility, Hanuman spoke, 'Respected Suryadev, I have heard that you are the world's best teacher. Sages from all over the universe come to your school to receive education. Would you be kind enough to admit me also to your school? I am eager to gain knowledge. I am prepared to face all challenges and hurdles.'

His attitude touched the master. Such students were rare to find. In fact, it was in his search for such diligent students the Sun God had started teaching. Right in the midst of his busy service of travelling around the universe offering sunlight, the Sun God took up a second optional vocation of teaching because of his passion for imparting knowledge to deserving candidates. Though he was happy to admit Hanuman to his school, there was a slight problem. The admissions were full.

He had begun a new batch with thousands of sages as fresh admissions. Since the only classroom in this school was his own chariot; just a limited number of students could be accommodated in his divine vehicle. And by this time, he had already reached the upper limit and there was no room for more. When he presented this problem to Hanuman, he just smiled. Where was the problem?

When the lessons began that day, the students in the classroom were shocked. There was a new student in class. No, that was not the cause of surprise. The shock was the new student wasn't sitting in the classroom, he was standing outside. As the classroom moved, so did the new student. He was flying at the speed of the chariot, while listening to the Sun God's lecture simultaneously. Amidst movements and rounds of shifting, Hanuman did not miss a single word that was being imparted and remained focussed. At some point, Hanuman became a little uncomfortable with the thought that while all the other students could see the face of their teacher, he had to fly parallel to the classroom. Thinking this to be a breach of etiquette, Hanuman turned around, faced the teacher and began flying backwards. The students were stunned, yet again. How could someone fly backwards and be so attentive at the same time?

Within the 60 orbits of the sun, Hanuman studied all the Vedas proficiently. The Sun God did not have to repeat even a single word. Every word that he spoke was permanently etched in Hanuman's mind. The Sun God was extremely impressed with his new student and embraced him and blessed him. Being grateful to his teacher for allowing him to study under his tutelage, Hanuman wanted to offer his master guru dakshina (formal expression of gratitude to a teacher).

The Sun God said, 'Hanuman, I am very impressed with your abilities, intelligence and your humble demeanour. I have never seen a student like you. If at all you wish to offer me guru dakshina, please do me a favour. My son Sugriva is in hiding. Bali has unjustly kidnapped his wife and kicked him out of his kingdom. The helpless Sugriva has taken shelter at the Mount Rishimukha to avoid facing Bali, since, that is the only place on Earth which is inaccessible to Bali. My son needs your able guidance. If you want to please me, I urge you to become Sugriva's minister and help him regain his kingdom.'

The Sun God never had to say anything twice to Hanuman. The Monkey God now stood as a wall between Sugriva and Bali. Not just a wall, but a fort...

Enthusiasm is the digester that helps assimilate any amount of knowledge.

Exhibition of ingratitude is the sign of indigestion of that knowledge.

A Flying Kick

'Why are you shivering like this?' He was surprised to see an absolutely normal person, suddenly, shivering like a dry leaf in the winds.

When no answer came from him, except for two drops of tears, Hanuman turned towards his three friends. Even the friends just looked down and seemed too ashamed to even answer this question.

This was weird. Why would four powerful Vanaras, who were extremely well-built and intelligent, behave like emotional, unconfident children? He kept questioning them and they kept turning away from him. Then, suddenly, it happened…

KRACCCKKK!

Hearing the sound, Hanuman turned to see Sugriva reeling in pain on the ground. All his friends were helping him recover. Hanuman just couldn't get it. What's going on here? What was that sound? How did Sugriva fall on the ground? Why was he holding his head in pain? Why were his friends unsurprised about the incident, almost as if, expecting it to happen as part of the daily routine?

By this time, Sugriva had recovered and he sat up. Still holding his head, he spoke, 'Hanuman, this happens 12 times, daily, at defined intervals.'

'What happens, Sugriva? Speak clearly.' Hanuman was intrigued by this untoward episode.

'My father, Surya, must have surely told you the story of my brother throwing me out of my kingdom and kidnapping my wife. But I don't think he would have shared another part to this story because it is too embarrassing for him as a father to come to terms with it. My brother, Bali, is cursed by Rishi Matanga that if he sets his feet on Mount Rishimukha, his head will crack open. That is the only reason I am still alive. Though the curse has saved my life, Bali has found his way to continue insulting and torturing me daily without even stepping on this hill.' Sugriva started shivering once again.

'It's time... It's time...' Sugriva was stammering in utter fear.

Hanuman turned away in disgust for a second. In that split second, something happened.

KRACCCKKK!

From the corner of his eyes, Hanuman could see that something had hit Sugriva on his head. Sugriva was on the floor, writhing in agony. Hanuman understood the seriousness of the matter that had to be handled with intelligence. He went and sat next to him to hear the complete story.

'Every day, Bali offers his oblations in the four oceans, to Surya, my father. With one leap he reaches from the southern ocean to the northern one and in another leap to the east and then to the west. Each time he leaps, he makes sure he passes over Mount Rishimukha and delivers a kick on my head and goes ahead. Three times a day, I receive four flying kicks from my brother. Though I know the exact time of the kick, I can't do anything to protect myself. Though my friends know that I am tortured like this every day, they are equally helpless in front of Bali's power. His speed and power are unmatchable. Before we can even see him, he disappears. In fact, the entire Kishkinda quakes in front of the power of Bali.' And Sugriva started trembling again.

This time, Hanuman was ready. Suddenly, he saw Bali zoom down with great speed, transferring all his energy into his feet to power pack his kick. As soon as Bali's feet reached just above the Sugriva's head, Hanuman caught both his feet with a single hand. Sugriva expecting a kick anytime soon had closed his eyes and shrunk. But when nothing happened, he slowly opened his eyes to see Bali's feet, above his head, dangling in the grip of Hanuman. Bali was stunned by Hanuman's audacity. No one had ever underestimated his strength. He jerked his feet with a little force to compel Hanuman to let go. He held on. Now, Bali put all his force. Still, he held on. Bali wondered who this monkey was.

That's when he saw the earrings made of five metals. He panicked. This was the very child he had tried to kill. He had heard of Hanuman's strength but never experienced it. By this time, Hanuman's grip on Bali's legs had intensified and it had begun to hurt Bali. Then Hanuman began pulling him downwards. Bali realised what he was attempting. He began to flutter at the very thought of it. He was somehow trying his best to get away from the grip of Hanuman but all his might was betraying him. Even the boon that he had of acquiring half the strength of his opponent in one glance seemed useless; it had no effect on Hanuman.

Soon, Sugriva and all the other monkeys realised what Hanuman was trying to do, they got excited and began to encourage Hanuman to throw Bali on the ground and allow his haughty head to crack. Understanding the precariousness of the situation, a helpless Bali began to plead with Hanuman. He promised never to return to Mount Rishimukha and trouble Sugriva. Considering his pitiful appeals, Hanuman let go.

As Bali flew away, Hanuman realised this was not a permanent solution. A more tangible solution had to be found or would the solution find them...

When you kick others at their weak point, time is timing a painful kick at your strong point.

The Perfectionist Beggar

'Bali is back!' A monkey came running at great speed and bumped into Hanuman.

How could Bali return so soon? Hanuman rose up to face the lurking danger. The danger had brought Sugriva and his four close associates together at a short notice. They followed the direction of his fingers to the edge of the cliff. Below Mount Rishimukha were stationed two muscular, broad-chested men, holding bows in their hands and walking together. The other four wondered where Bali was. Trying to decipher their quizzical looks, Sugriva explained these two men had been sent by Bali to annihilate him.

Looking at Hanuman, Sugriva instructed, 'Go in disguise and ascertain who these two men are. If they are Bali's men, then let me prepare for my death. With powerful men as enemies, my survival is impossible. However, if they are not Bali's allies, then bring them to me, we should propose a pact of friendship and use them as instruments to crush Bali.'

Disguised as a bikshuk sanyasi (mendicant), Hanuman walked down the hill towards the two handsome-looking ascetic warriors. Soon, he was standing in front of them.

When he first gazed at them, something began to happen inside him. He felt that his bones were melting. He wasn't able to speak or even think for a while. He couldn't understand what was happening to him. Soon, recollecting the purpose of his visit, he began to speak.

'Who are you, mighty heroes? Where are you heading? Though dressed as ascetics, your beauty and power would put the gods to shame. Seeing your mighty bows which resemble rainbows, who wouldn't be mesmerised? Confidence oozes out of your lion-like gait. You are destined to rule kingdoms, and not take on the role of ascetics. The combination of sweetness and power convinces me that you are extraordinary people here, on an extraordinary mission. Could I have the honour of knowing more about you?'

Smiling at him, one of them spoke, 'We will answer your questions soon; first tell us, how can a beggar with tattered clothes wear such a rare and precious diamond necklace?'

As soon as Hanuman heard that question, he almost fainted with joy. He instantly recalled Lord Brahma's words he had heard in his childhood. This was his Lord and Master for whom he had waited all his life. As soon as this realisation dawned on him, he shed his disguise and appeared in his original form. When asked for his introduction, Hanuman immediately announced, 'I am Sugriva's minister.'

Upon uttering these words, he immediately realised he had committed a grave mistake. He noticed a slight movement; his Lord had taken one step back and allowed his brother to step forward to introduce them. The brother spoke, 'This is Rama, the son of King Dasharatha of Ayodhya. The world knows me as his brother, Lakshmana. But I consider myself to be his worthy servant. We have been exiled from our kingdom for 14 years and have spent our last

13 years in the forest of Dandakaranya. Unfortunately, Sita, Lord Rama's wife has been kidnapped by a demon named Ravana and we are here in search of her.'

Hanuman cursed himself for having declared himself to be Sugriva's minister. After hearing Lakshmana's humble introduction, he felt even worse. He decided to amend his mistake with time. Hanuman invited them to make an alliance with Sugriva, who was also in a similar situation, after having lost his wife and kingdom to Bali.

When Hanuman stepped away for a moment to inform Sugriva of their arrival, Lord Rama analysed the speech of Hanuman and shared his observations with Lakshmana. He said, 'Did you hear Hanuman's speech? The charm of his voice was amazing. He used the right words at the right time. He was pleasing, gentle and had gravitas. The content of his speech comforted the heart.

'In order to speak like this, he must be well-versed with the Rg, Yajur and Sama Vedas. He couldn't have been this gentle had he not studied these Vedas. He must have learnt from able teachers. Knowledge of the *Rg Veda* makes one humble and also gives one the power to recall and reproduce that knowledge. Knowledge of the *Yajur Veda* sharpens memory. Knowledge of the *Sama Veda* assures musical perfection and every word becomes like a song. Surely, he has perfected Vyakarana or grammar; there was absolutely no mistake in his joining of sentences.

'He spoke so much, yet, he did not use even one wrong word. His speech was so perfect that he began at a certain speed and volume and ended at the same speed and volume. He knew which words should be spoken from the stomach or pronounced from the palate and where to use the nose in his speech. While speaking, not for once there was a shift in his focus. Without a controlled mind, one cannot stop misusing words. His speech has the ability to win over an enemy armed with an upraised sword. If I get such a person as an associate, I can achieve success.'

Mounting on Hanuman's broad shoulders, Lord Rama and Lakshmana began their ascent to the peak of Mount Rishimukha. Both of them were deeply appreciative of this person. However, Hanuman was lost in thought, worried about rectifying the one mistake he'd made earlier in the day. He decided that sensitivity was the only way to deal with an insensitive mistake. He was ready for rectification as much as Sugriva was eager for confrontation…

Under the watchful eyes of a genuine guide, one's pretentions melt and hidden qualities shape up.

Speech is the air that brings out the odour of your heart. Fine speech with the right intention reveals an aromatic heart. Harsh speech with sarcasm denotes a smelly heart. Confused speech with denial of responsibility symbolises a depressed heart.

A Friend's Betrayal

As the three reached up the cliff, they were face-to-face with Sugriva who stood with his hands on his hips, carefully observing the new entrants. Hanuman bent on his knees and allowed the brothers to unmount. The two parties were introduced to each other.

Understanding Lord Rama's situation and clearly identifying with it, Sugriva extended his hand and welcomed Lord Rama as his newly found friend. Lord Rama gracefully accepted his reception and returned the gesture by extending his own hands. As they shook hands like long-standing friends, Hanuman shook his head in disgust. He was thinking, how could Sugriva not understand that Rama is their worshipable Lord and shouldn't be treated as a mere friend?

After giving them a tour of the scenic Mount Rishimukha, Sugriva brought them to the centre of the mountaintop and pulled out a huge branch from a Sal tree. Placing it down, he offered it as a seat for Lord Rama. Lord Rama obliged and sat on one side of the branch. Sugriva took his place on the other side, turning a blind eye to

Lakshmana. Hanuman struck his head in disgust seeing this act of insensitivity. Even Lord Rama noticed this grave mistake and felt bad.

Hanuman quickly jumped and pulled down the branch of a much better tree, a sandalwood tree. Placing it next to Lord Rama's side, he offered the seat to Lakshmana. As soon as Lakshmana seated himself, Hanuman sat on the floor next to Lakshmana. He didn't feel eligible to acquire a place beside Lakshmana, let alone occupy a place next to Lord Rama. Lord Rama was mighty impressed by Hanuman's sensitivity.

To teach Sugriva a lesson in humility and also as punishment for disrespecting Lakshmana, Lord Rama sent Sugriva to fight Bali. The timid brother was brutally beaten up in the duel. Later, the excuse he gave for not being able to kill Bali was that the siblings looked similar. Lord Rama requested Lakshmana to garland Sugriva so that it could serve as a differentiator between the two brothers. When Sugriva bent to receive the garland from Lakshmana, Lord Rama considered that to be his act of forgiveness. This time, Lord Rama didn't allow Sugriva to suffer at the hands of Bali.

With Bali becoming history, Sugriva was appointed the King of Kishkinda. With *kingly* power came *kingly* enjoyment and royal forgetfulness...

Where power and sensitivity coexist, success and relationships live in harmony.

A Forgotten Commitment

'Come out, Sugriva. You foolish monkey!' A ball of fire was swinging back and forth in front of Sugriva's palace.

'You ungrateful wretch! How can you enjoy yourself when your friend suffers?' The soldiers of Sugriva didn't know how to respond to this person. They thought his confidence level was too high because he called their master by his first name, that too, casually. They decided to stay away from the King's personal matters, especially, since the King was not responding at all. At least, he should have given them a signal what was expected of them.

Initially, Sugriva avoided responding to the abuse, but when it was persistent he couldn't tolerate any more. It was a question of his repute in front of his subjects. From the corner of his bedroom window, when Sugriva glanced at Lakshmana, he understood his fury. In order to pacify an enraged Lakshmana, he sent the intelligent Tara. Tara did manage to control his temper.

Once Lakshmana calmed down, Sugriva ventured forth. By this time, Hanuman had also joined them. Hanuman knew Lakshmana was a man of fewer words and more actions. If he were left to handle this alone, Sugriva would not stand a chance. Hanuman spoke to Sugriva, reminding him of his promise. He said, 'For the last four months, Lord Rama has been patiently waiting for you to begin helping him. You have been enjoying in your palace with your wives, whereas Lord Rama has been suffering in isolation, separated from his beloved. At the outset, the monsoon was the pretext for your inaction, but now, the rains are long gone. Why are you procrastinating? Don't you remember how swiftly Lord Rama killed Bali and saved your life? Has over-indulgence in sensual pleasures made your mind dull? Don't you know who Lord Rama is? It is for your own good that I suggest you seek refuge in Lord Rama and beg for forgiveness for the indefinite delay. Lord Rama is very kind, he will definitely forgive you. Ungratefulness is greater than the greatest of vices. My dear King, get rid of ungratefulness and embrace lasting prosperity.'

Hanuman's speech invoked the spirit of dedication and compassion in Sugriva and he got over his inertia within moments. He was ready to do his best. In no time, Sugriva deployed his soldiers and gave the necessary orders. Soon, monkeys began to pour into Kishkinda in millions. A search operation was underway...

Silent gratitude develops into audible commitment when the happiness of getting a favour is replaced by the desire to return it.

Consistency in commitment is easy when the depth of gratitude is high.

A Trustworthy Hero

The eagle panicked for a moment seeing what it saw below. A new sea. How could a new sea appear overnight? Puzzled, the eagle dived in to test the waters. Soon, it panicked; it was not a sea it was an army!

Every colour, every size and every form could be seen. The numbers were so huge that one could easily mistake it for a swirling ocean, if seen from way above. This was the monkey army of Sugriva, the King of Kishkinda. His brother had left behind a kingdom much bigger than what any monkey could comprehend. This army was the factual proof of that. As soon as a high command had been issued from the land of Kishkinda, these millions of monkeys from across the world had poured in overnight.

Sugriva, the new King, deftly divided the army into four parts appointing a leader for each segment. Each division was assigned an area in order to carry out the operation. The search for Sita began with great enthusiasm. Each party had been given a few ornaments in order to convince her about their genuinity. Of the four divisions, the segment which had Angada as the leader comprised other stalwarts including the wise Jambavan and the hero Hanuman. With these three mighty supermen in the team, it was quite obvious that their best bet was the southern direction which they were assigned. Though Lord Rama had greeted and thanked everybody in advance for their efforts, he personally chose to meet only Hanuman.

This was an epic moment for Hanuman. When he heard that Lord Rama wanted to meet in private, he couldn't believe it. For the last four months, from the time he had made the stupid, yet inadvertent, mistake of declaring himself to be Sugriva's servant, Lord Rama had withdrawn from him with a sense of disappointment. He had desperately tried his best to please the Lord with his behaviour and actions. But, all that didn't seem to have the desired effect on the Lord. However, this call was a confirmation that it did have a subtle effect. Hanuman realised that nothing he did ever went unnoticed by Lord Rama.

With great joy in his heart, Hanuman rushed to meet his Lord. Rama was seated on a rock, peering at something which He held in his hands. Though, Hanuman couldn't see what He was holding from his vantage point, he quickly realised that whatever it was, it had to be something Lord Rama's life revolved around.

When Hanuman kneeled down, next to the Lord, He said something that remained etched in his heart. 'Hanuman, I have great confidence in your abilities. If there is anyone who can find Sita, it is you. Therefore, I am giving you a ring that symbolises our eternal bond,' the Lord pleaded.

Lord Rama then handed over the ring to Hanuman. 'This ring represents Sita's innocence,' added Lord Rama. He narrated an incident that was known only to Him and Sita. He said, 'One day, Sita was massaging My feet. Suddenly, she removed this ring from her finger and threw it on the floor. When I asked her the reason for this odd behaviour, she said something that fascinated Me. She said that the last time an ordinary granite stone touched Your feet, it transformed into the most beautiful woman on earth, Ahalya. What if the diamond stone on this ring comes in contact with the same feet? She was sure that it would get transformed into a superlative form of beauty. She didn't want a competitor; she wanted no other source of distraction, more beautiful than her. It was then that Sita threw the stone ring away.'

By this time, Lord Rama had tears welling up in His eyes. He went on to describe how Sita had no idea what a forest looked like. She wasn't even able to comprehend where the city ended and where the forest began. He wondered how the innocent angel would survive in the land of crooked demons. Lord Rama then went on to describe the beauty of every limb of Sita to help Hanuman identify her. Lord Rama's description was so vivid that anyone could get completely bewitched by the charm of Sita.

Though, Hanuman was a celibate and had never seen a woman—beyond her feet—in his life, Lord Rama's description of His wife's beauty was immaculate. The premise of Lord Rama's revelation was trust. In the brief period of four months, Hanuman had won over the trust of Lord Rama. With this one act, Lord Rama had revealed to the world what spotless character meant and what is the end result of good education. According to Lord Rama, Hanuman was a person of integrity whom He could trust with anything and everything.

Confidence doesn't necessarily mean completion of a task, trust doesn't really mean accomplishment; life is a struggle to find the truth.

Your trustworthiness quotient depends on your transparency ratio.

The Lost Brother

Famished! Exhausted! Dying!

The monkeys that ventured in the southern direction could think of nothing else except these three words. It had been close to a month and they had earned no clue of Sita's whereabouts. They weren't even sure if she lived at all. Some of the monkeys, frustrated with hunger, began to question the purpose of the project. 'Why are we wasting our time searching for one woman? Is she so precious that so many of us have to sacrifice our lives for her sake?' These were the common discussions that took place in the lower ranks. The leaders hadn't yet given up. The mission would die a premature death the day their leaders gave up.

Exactly when the monkey entourage was on the verge of losing some of its men, Jambavan saw a bird flying out of a cave. How was that possible? He shook his head and rubbed his eyes to carefully look again. Yes, it was true.

The surprise was that not only was it an aquatic bird, but, that it was wet—dripping wet. There had to be a source of water within the cave. The difference between living and dying was one word—water. And here it was.

A new wave of enthusiasm engulfed the search party and they ran joyously towards the cave, shouting and hooting. At the entrance, they realised it was much bigger than regular caves. The entire troupe entered. Soon, they found their source of water. Just when they were about to dive, they spotted a woman sitting on its bank. She looked grave and was dressed like an exalted ascetic. Sensing their presence through her yogic trance, she opened her eyes. As soon as she opened her eyes, a golden table appeared in front of them. The table was filled with the most palatable delicacies the monkeys had ever seen. There were innumerable varieties of dishes and celestial beverages. With her hands, the ascetic lady who introduced herself as Svayamprabha, signalled them to commence the feast. Wholeheartedly, the monkeys devoured the meal. They ate more than they could handle. Each monkey was filled to the brim with happiness.

Suddenly, everything vanished. They found themselves lying on the sands next to the ocean shore. Where were they? How did they reach here? What had happened to the food? Who was that lady? None of them had a clue as to what was happening with them. They had lost all sense of direction. There wasn't anyone in the vicinity to ask for help. Again, a dead end.

Days passed and no one was able to decipher anything. The effect of the meal they'd had at the cave was now wearing off. They were hungry and thirsty again. This time, no wet bird and no cave with delicious food was at their disposal. They were losing all hope. The monkeys began praying earnestly for some help or some intervention. Angad spoke, 'What is the point in living anymore? A few days left before the month gets over. Sadly, we still haven't been able to find

Mother Sita. How can we go back with no information? It's better to die than to return empty-handed.'

'KEEEELLLLLL!KEEEEELLLLL!KEEEEELLLLL!'

All of them gazed skywards. There was an old, giant vulture hovering above them. Clearly, it was a sign. A sign of their imminent death. The vulture was waiting for its first victim. The first victim would be its food. Looking at Hanuman, Angad said, 'Doesn't this vulture look like Jatayu who heroically sacrificed his life trying to save Mother Sita from Ravana's clutches? Jatayu was fortunate to have been cremated by Lord Rama himself. I don't think Lord Rama will ever find our bodies after this vulture unleashes its terror on us.'

As soon as Angad spoke those words, the monkeys began to run away. Angad couldn't understand why his army was going helter-skelter. He looked up and saw that the giant vulture, which had been hovering way above them, was now fast rushing towards him. Even before Angad could react, the vulture landed right next to him hurling a sand storm in his direction, with the fluttering of its wings. Once he settled down, Angad could see a look of concern in the bird's eyes, without any vicious intent.

'Do you know Jatayu? He was my younger brother. Years ago, we got separated due to a mishap and we never met again. My name is Sampati. I am saddened to learn of Jatayu's death. I saw that evil Ravana, the killer of my brother, carrying Mother Sita away to Lanka which is located 100 yojana (1 yojana is equivalent to 8 miles) from here, across the ocean. In fact, with my powerful vision, I can see Mother Sita in Lanka right now. When I got separated from my brother, my wings had been charred and I couldn't fly long distances. At that time, a sage told me that the day

I tell a group of monkeys the whereabouts of Mother Sita, my wings will grow back.'

Mourning the loss of his brother and encouraging the monkey army to not give up and instead try reaching Lanka, Sampati flew away. He gave them a solution, but, his solution led them to a greater problem. Who will cross a 100-yojana ocean?

> *Embracing negativity is equivalent to embracing failure.*
> *Mining diamonds is the art of spotting the positivity in a deeply negative environment.*

The Making of a Superhero

The question was not whether they wanted to do it. The question was whether they could. Faced with a newfound problem, the monkeys began to offer their bid. It was definitely a gamble. The gamble of life. All the monkeys in the army were sincerely trying to showcase their strength and present their best skills in this match. Everyone comes to gamble with good intentions, but the winning question is not whether you have the right intention, but whether your ability and action support your intention?

One monkey said that he could jump 1 yojana. Another said he could jump 2 yojana. Yet another quipped that he could easily cover 12 yojana. An even more adventurous one declared 65 yojana. Finally, Angad, the son of the powerful hero Bali said, he could cover the entire stretch of 100 yojana himself. His grand claim led to a buzz of excitement in the army. There was a brave warrior in the army who was confident about his abilities. However, the excitement died as soon as he uttered, 'But... What now?'

Angad continued, 'The problem is though I can cover 100 yojana in one go and reach Lanka, I surely wouldn't have the strength to return.'

Jambavan, their leader, who wasn't a monkey like the rest but a bear, spoke up. 'In my younger days, I had so much energy that I could cover the universe several times over. In fact, when Vaamanadev appeared and extended his leg to cover the whole universe, I used that opportunity to circumambulate, thus actually orbiting the entire universe 21 times. But, I am old now and don't have the same strength and energy. I don't think I would be able to cross this 100-yojana ocean. Time does humble everyone.'

Silence prevailed. Each one of them had put forth their concern, but still, they couldn't arrive at a sensible conclusion. Dejected, they all lowered their heads in shame and started brooding over their inabilities. The leader in Jambavan rose to the occasion. He realised that each one of them was only thinking from their point of view and none of them were analysing the strength of the others. Jambavan began analysing the strengths and weaknesses of each monkey in all the sections. By now, he knew his team well. As he continued his examination, he came across one monkey who had not spoken at all. He was lost in his thoughts. Suddenly, he realised this monkey could accomplish this incredible task. The silent monkey was Hanuman.

Jambavan sat next to Hanuman and reminded him of what he had forgotten. He gently reminded him of all the powers that the demigods had bestowed on him when he was a child. He reminded him of his super-human abilities. He reminded him of his greatness. He reminded him that when great powers are bestowed on someone, it means greater responsibility rests on him. Power and responsibility go hand in hand. Now that he was standing on the shores of responsibility, his powers were bound to return.

As Jambavan spoke, Hanuman began recollecting his lost and forgotten powers. There was a rise in his confidence level. Soon, he began to grow in size. Within moments, Hanuman was a few hundred feet tall. The other monkeys looked up in amazement at the sudden transformation of their friend. Hanuman roared. The intensity was such that the trees quaked and birds fluttered in all directions.

The Monkey God began running towards Mount Mahendra, covering the distance in a few strides. Climbing the mountain in easy steps, he reached the peak in a flash. Standing right at its summit, he yelled, 'Victory to Lord Rama! Jai Shri Rama! There is nothing that I can't do. Nothing can stop me from achieving success in my Lord's mission!'

He prepared for the big leap. Gathering all his energy in his feet, he put immense pressure on the mountain on which he stood. The mountain was squashed under his weight and streams of gold, silver and many minerals began to flow out in different directions. Sages began running out of the caves from the mountain and animals began to move away from the pressure points and move closer to Hanuman's feet.

Abruptly, Hanuman jumped and took off from the mountain. The power of his jump created a suction force that dragged everything in the vicinity of his feet skywards. Elephants, lions, deer, rabbits, birds, plants and trees started trailing Hanuman. They flew along for a little distance till the suction lasted and then fell back on the mountain. It appeared as if Hanuman was their guest and they had gone along with him to see him off as he proceeded on his journey to Lanka.

Jumping off the mountain was one thing and reaching Lanka was quite another. Reaching Lanka was not a matter of jumping across the ocean. On the 100-yojana stretch, there were some explosives that were strategically placed to make the journey eventful.

The achievement of making an achiever is far greater than the achievement of becoming an achiever.

Encouraging Jambavans create achieving Hanumans. For the world, the achiever is the hero. For the achiever, the one who made him an achiever is the hero.

Hanuman Can Fly!

A monkey's ambitious flight was an incredible sight for all.

A host of demigods joyfully observed the determined Hanuman flying across the ocean. Some of them felt they should help him while others wanted to test him. The two parties left in different directions.

A little ahead, Hanuman could see something glittering in the ocean. However, due to the distance, it was difficult to make out what it was. As he edged closer, the unidentified object seemed to grow rapidly in size. Soon, Hanuman saw a golden mountain rising from inside the ocean. The colossal golden mountain almost touched the skies and blocked Hanuman's path. He couldn't see a thing beyond the massive mountain.

Hovering, he inspected the freshly arisen mountain. Scenic lakes, succulent fruit-bearing trees, healing herbs, beautiful gardens, comfortable seating arrangements, birds and animals meandered around. The mountain looked like paradise. Right at the centre of the mountain, almost at par with Hanuman's height, appeared a brilliantly effulgent personality who stood with folded hands, looking intently towards him.

He spoke in a voice that had the power of thunder and, yet, the sweetness of a flowing river. 'My dear hero, I am here on the orders of the great demigods who are impressed with your prowess and determination to serve Lord Rama. I am Mount Mainaka. Long back, Indra, the King of the Heavens went on a rampage destroying the mountains of the world. During that era, all the mountains had wings. We could freely fly from one place to another. Unfortunately, a few proud mountains took advantage of this faculty and landed themselves on human civilisations, causing mass destruction. That's when Indra decided to clip the wings of all mountains, making them immobile.

'When I saw Indra coming after me with thunderbolt in his hands, I panicked and began to shiver. The demigod in-charge of the oceans, Varuna, showered his kindness upon me and blew me far away from Indra's tyranny. He arranged for my safety within the depths of his vast oceans. Today, on seeing your heroic efforts, Varuna has asked me to receive you on my mountains and be hospitable to you so that you feel rejuvenated before proceeding on your challenging journey. I personally feel that by serving you, I will get a chance to reciprocate the kindness Varuna had bestowed upon me ages ago. Kindly come and purify my mountains by your saintly visit.'

Hanuman smiled at the tempting request. Thanking him, he said, 'The word "rest" does not feature in my dictionary when I am on a mission. Though, I must confess it's an irresistible offer. Unfortunately, I can't wait for a second longer. I cannot think of my own comforts till the mission is complete. The only concern that governs my thoughts is Lord Rama's well-being. Perhaps, on my return, once my mission is accomplished, I may consider your invitation. For now, I must move on.'

Not to appear insensitive and rude, Hanuman touched the mountain with his hands accepting his service and flew away. Mount Mainaka was rendered speechless at Hanuman's dedication.

Comfort is a highway robber that loots us of our achievements.

As Hanuman continued flying way above the ocean, he admired the serene waters. Suddenly, a little further ahead, he could see the ocean develop suction current. Something inside the water was creating it. The next instant, a fountain of water was thrown skywards and the ocean surface became agitated. Hanuman slowed down to determine the cause of the disturbance. With a huge splash, from within the waters emerged a gigantic demoness who had the face of a human but the trunk of a python. This was Surasa, the mother of the Nagas, in her most terrifying form.

She spoke, hissing like a snake, 'Hssss... No one can bypassssssss me. I have Brahmasssssss' boon that anyone who passes over me will become my natural food and enter my belly. Today, you are my meal. No one can sssssstop that now...'

Surasa opened her mouth wide enough, to devour Hanuman in one gulp. As soon as her mouth became as big as Hanuman, suction began to pull the monkey towards it. Hanuman resisted the pull and expanded himself a bit. When Surasa saw what Hanuman was trying to do, she also began to expand her mouth to beat Hanuman. Soon, Hanuman was 10 yojana in height. Surasa expanded her mouth to become 20 yojana. Hanuman stretched more and became 30 yojana, while, she turned 40 yojana. The tussle continued till Hanuman stopped at 80 and Surasa at 100 yojana.

In a flash, Hanuman shrunk himself to the size of a fly while her mouth remained 100 yojana wide. He dashed into her mouth and slid through her tongue. He glided all the way into her throat and entered her belly. On reaching her belly, he flew up and came out from her mouth again and assumed his regular size. Surasa could feel something enter her mouth, reach her belly and exit. But, it all happened so fast that she hardly had any time to react. By the time she realised it was Hanuman who had tricked her, he had already made his exit.

With folded hands, Hanuman stood in front of her and spoke in a heart-melting voice. 'My dear mother, I have honoured the words of Lord Brahma. I have entered your belly and come out. You shouldn't have any complaint against me now. Kindly bless me and permit me to proceed on my journey to find Mother Sita.'

Hanuman's intelligence brought great joy to Surasa. She was, in fact, thrilled with the experience of interacting with Hanuman. Blessing him profusely, she disappeared happily.

Once competition gets over, real growth takes place.

A free Hanuman began to soar into the sky, yet again. This time, he hoped there would be no new obstacles. Time was running out and the pressure was mounting. Surasa had wasted sufficient time in competing with him unnecessarily. Of course, he was happy he did not disrespect her. Blessings were important in any venture, especially, in unpredictable missions of life, like the one he was on.

Suddenly, something went wrong… Terribly wrong.

Though his mind raced, his body had stalled. He wasn't able to move forward. He was suspended in thin air. This was strange. It felt as if someone had caught him, though, no one was visible. Suddenly, he was being dragged downwards. A free fall ensued. He had no idea what was happening and who was controlling his movements. He was desperately looking around for the cause. Unless he knew what the cause was, what was he supposed to do?

Observing the ocean water, he discovered something interesting. His own shadow. Someone was holding down his shadow. He could clearly see a huge hand encircling his shadow, pulling it downwards into the ocean. Instantly, it struck him there was some evil force that was directing his movements by controlling his shadow. He was aware of such powers but actually saw it in action for the first time. He was fast approaching the ocean surface. He knew that as soon as he would hit the surface, the shadow puller would do the needful. He didn't have much time to plan his next course of action.

Without any warning, the calm surface of the water split and a huge monster emerged with her mouth wide open. With her entry, a thunderous voice from the sky proclaimed, 'Simhika!' Hanuman recognised the name immediately. She was the demoness Sugriva had warned him about. She was the greatest fear for anyone who tried reaching Lanka. Ravana had purposefully kept her hungry, so she wouldn't spare anyone trying to gain access to Lanka. Her wide mouth was filled with countless razor-sharp teeth.

Instantly, Hanuman shrunk himself to the size of a fly and entered her mouth. Next, he extended both his hands and held them far out. As he slid into her throat, the ten fingers of his hands, which had sharp nails, began to slice through her organs. He, systematically, entered every corner of her body and ripped apart all the essential organs. Initially, Simhika was happy that Hanuman turned out to be such an easy prey. She began to focus on digesting him. Suddenly, she started feeling intense pain in different parts of her body. She realised something was wrong inside her. She was in agony now.

Hanuman completed his job in a few minutes and decided to make his exit plan. Tearing open her stomach, he rushed out. As soon as he flew out of her body, Simhika collapsed with blood pouring out from her mouth and her ruptured stomach. As Hanuman hovered above, looking at Simhika sink into the ocean bed, hundreds of sharks attacked her body, devouring her flesh. The ocean turned red in no time.

After overcoming the last obstacle, Hanuman valiantly moved towards his destination. Lanka was now only minutes away. But Mother Sita still seemed hours away...

The school of envy teaches you that others' failure is your success.

The school of humility teaches you that envying others' success is your real failure.

A Punching Entry

The aerial view of Lanka was picturesque. Surrounded, from all directions, by beautiful beaches, lush green forests, the devil's abode was a heavenly sight. Hanuman marvelled at the topography of Lanka. Beyond the beaches, there was a mountainous forest. Within the forest was installed a huge golden wall that safeguarded the city of Lanka from all kinds of attacks and intrusions. Landing on a mountaintop, Hanuman patiently waited for nightfall in order to plan his first move.

A cat stealthily walked up to the golden gate of the golden city. The cat was careful not to meow. Looking around, it made a dash towards the gate at the opportune moment while the stationed guards crossed each other. Managing to jump between the bars, the cat entered the golden city of Lanka. So much for stringent security...

'Who are you?' a voice roared while a huge javelin was thrust blocking the cat's onward movement. The cat was taken aback. This was least expected, especially, after having crossed the front gate without much trouble. Looking up, he saw a pair of dangerous-looking red eyes staring at him in anger. Now, there was no point in hiding his true form.

Surprised at the cat transforming into a powerful-looking monkey prince, she spoke, 'I am Lankini, the Goddess of Lanka. No one enters Lanka without my sanction and King Ravana's permission. Since you dared the impossible, you have to face the consequences.'

She quickly delivered a swift slap on Hanuman's face. No one had hit him this way. Outraged at being attacked like this, he roared and clenched his right fist. He hurled a blow that sent her reeling in pain. She fell at a distance with a thud, remaining immobile for a while.

When she got up, she had tears in her eyes and her countenance had completely changed. She wasn't the wild demoness anymore and had taken on the role of a helpless victim. With folded hands, she came in front of Hanuman and kneeled before him in supplication. She said, 'Long back, Lord Brahma had told me, the day a monkey punches me, it would mark the beginning of the end of Lanka. Now, I know for sure that Ravana will soon be history. I bless you and may you achieve success in your mission. Lord Rama shall be victorious.'

Hanuman's punch had always triggered devastation. For the first time, he was surprised to witness a transformation in a demoness. He was happy to punch more if such were the results.

The gates of Lanka had opened for him with a punch. Could he open the gates of his luck with a punch as well? He needed luck by his side to find Mother Sita in such a huge and heavily guarded empire.

Wisdom is the art of delivering the right punch line to transform ignorance into mindfulness.

Is This Sita?

A stroll through Lanka had been nothing less than a stroll through the heavens. Every corner of the land was exquisite. The palaces were simmering with golden bricks—used abundantly—studded with gems of various colours and types. Landscaped gardens were strewn across the city adding charm to the magnificent architecture. Music added flavour to the different varieties of entertainment-theme parks that dotted the city. The most beautiful building of all was Ravana's residential palace that was carved out of pure gold. Paradise would be an understatement to capture the essence of what the palace represented in one word.

With the hope of finding Mother Sita, Hanuman, assuming a tiny form, cautiously moved around the inner chambers of Ravana's palace. He was surprised to see the number of women that were strolling around the inner bedroom chambers of Ravana in a drunken state. Most of them were scantily clothed. When he peeped into the innermost section of the gigantic chamber, he gasped. There, on an enormous bed, was lying Dasanana, the majestic King of Lanka. The first look at Ravana brought out mixed emotions in Hanuman's heart. He was awestruck at Ravana's grandeur. Blessed with extremely handsome looks, a perfectly chiselled body, complemented with an enviable intelligence, Ravana deserved appreciation. But, all that Hanuman could feel for him was disgust at his lack of virtues.

Leaving Ravana aside, Hanuman began to gaze around trying to spot Mother Sita. Suddenly, his eyes fell on a woman who was lying on Ravana's splendid bed. Looking at her beauty, Hanuman felt this must be Mother Sita. Her features resembled the description Lord Rama shared with him. He felt overjoyed for having accomplished his mission. But, then, something didn't seem right. How could Mother Sita be on Ravana's bed? He began to analyse to ascertain the truth.

He saw her mumbling something in her sleep. When he heard carefully, he could hear her speaking a lot of inauspicious things. This couldn't be Mother Sita. The only words that could possibly come out of Mother Sita's mouth were the names of Lord Rama and the auspicious glorification of the lord's qualities. Moreover, Mother Sita would never be able to eat or sleep peacefully without Lord Rama's presence in her life. Why would she decorate herself for another male, thought Hanuman? This, definitely, couldn't be Mother Sita.

Then, he saw two things that reconfirmed his suspicion. There was no auspicious Padma Line (a special mark) on the sole of her feet and there was no marking of a lotus flower on her toe. These were supposed to be the emblems on the body of the Goddess of Fortune, Mother Sita. Further, Hanuman also noted that the vermilion from her forehead had been rubbed off indicating her husband wouldn't live for long. This couldn't be Mother Sita, but had to be Mandodari, the Chief Queen of Ravana.

Concluding thus, he began to observe the other thousands of women who lay in Ravana's harem. Suddenly, an uncomfortable thought struck him. What was he doing staring at semi-nude women in someone else's bedroom? Wasn't he supposed to be a celibate who was to abstain from even looking at women?

Hanuman reflected on the purpose of his visit. The motive determines whether an act is virtuous or sinful. If he had to find Mother Sita, he had to look around carefully. For the success of any mission, there has to be some austerity practised. In his mission, looking at women was the austerity he had to tolerate. As long as he was not looking at them with the desire of 'enjoying' them, he wasn't violating any principle. Once this was clear in his mind, Hanuman continued his search.

Soon, he realised that none of them were Mother Sita. Mother Sita was as powerful as fire and couldn't be kept subdued for long. Ravana had to keep her far away from his valuable possessions. The question was, where?

Determination is born out of desperation.
Resignation is born out of complacency.

The Dead End

Every corner of Lanka had been explored. Every palace had been checked. Every street had been scanned. Every secret hideout had been investigated. Still, there was no sign of the divine lady.

Hanuman was at his wits' end. He had no idea where Mother Sita was and had no clue how to proceed. Worry began to overpower his calm mind. He began to consider the most extreme possibilities. Could Ravana have devoured her, knowing she wouldn't submit to him? Could she have fallen into the ocean in transit? Could it be that she gave up her life after months of separation from Lord Rama?

Hanuman felt dispirited. He shrunk into a dark corner of Lanka. Horrible images of the consequences of his failure began to flash on the screen of his disturbed mind. Thousands of monkeys were awaiting his successful return. The first trace of news of his failure in Lanka would lead to their tragic death. The fatal end of his army would cause Sugriva to give up his life knowing he had failed to keep his promise to Lord Rama. Upon Surgiva's death, Lord Rama would not be able to live after losing all hope of finding Sita. With Lord Rama's demise, Lakshmana would not survive a minute longer. Ayodhya would turn into a crematorium. Imagining mass annihilation as an outcome of his failure, Hanuman felt there was no point in pulling on the agony. A despondent Hanuman wanted to end his life.

Seeing a dead end in every direction, Hanuman decided to take complete solace in Lord Rama's holy names. As he began chanting Lord Rama's names fervently, something interesting happened. Chandra, the moon, till then, hidden behind a set of clouds peeped out. It seemed as if Chandra was interested in knowing who was chanting the names of Lord Rama. Chandra's rays revealed something that excited Hanuman. Down below was a valley that was completely hidden from the world. Though he had searched all of Lanka, he had completely missed this spot.

As he glanced in that direction, he realised this was the most beautiful area in Lanka. This had to be the place where Ravana had held Mother Sita captive. He ran in that direction with great enthusiasm and newly found hope. As he ran, a realisation dawned in his mind, a dead end actually ends the illusion that you are in control of your goal and forces you to take shelter in higher powers that shine brilliantly and are eager to give you a definite direction.

Prayer is a torchlight that shows you hidden possibilities in the dark environment of your despondent mind.

Mother Sita Found

Today, he realised the meaning of gold-covered dust. Under the Ashoka tree shone a brilliant streak of golden light covered by forest dust. Quickly recollecting the description, given to him by Lord Rama, he deciphered that this had to be Mother Sita that millions of monkeys were searching for across the globe. Draped in a single cloth, her body appeared emaciated with months of fasting and her face had moistened with rivers of tears running down her cheeks. This goddess was an epitome of virtue and chastity.

Surrounding this innocent lady were hundreds of vicious-looking, one-eyed and one-eared demonesses. On counting closely, Hanuman realised they were 700 in total. This was an age-old trick that demons adopted to break their tough captives into submission—surround them with ugly, fierce-looking monsters—and constantly harass them with abusive words and threatening actions. The human mind naturally cannot handle so much negativity. Sita wasn't any ordinary human, obviously, and her determination had not faltered even a bit. But, Hanuman realised that she was definitely on the verge of breaking down due to constant torture and abuse.

Just then, a series of drumbeats woke up everyone. Suddenly, Ashok Vatika was bustling with action. Hanuman hid himself in the foliage of the tall tree he was seated on. Announcements were made heralding the arrival of the King of Lanka. Basking under the brilliant morning sun, Ravana walked in majestically, accompanied by an entourage carrying hundreds of golden plates covered with silken cloth. There was an air of enthusiasm and excitement around Ravana. He almost appeared like a smitten youth walking up to propose to the girl he'd given his heart to.

'O Sita, please accept these exquisite gifts that I have procured for your pleasure. No one in this world will be able to offer you valuables like these. I have even got the finest cuisines to enliven your taste buds. I only request you to accept me as your master. Forget that aimless wanderer Rama. He has nothing to offer you anymore. You know very well that Rama won't even be able to find you, let alone rescue you. Submit to me and enjoy the pleasures of life. Don't let your precious youth go waste.' Ravana was commanding and begging her at the same time.

Suddenly, Sita's face became taut. She was no more the vulnerable, soft lady who was on the verge of breaking down.

Determination sparkled vividly on her face now. Hanuman was impressed with this instant change. Even from a distance, he could clearly make out the contours of her face changing from helplessness to disgust. She shouted at Ravana in a manner that seemingly shocked the meek loyal servants of the emperor.

'These petty gifts cannot impress me, O Ravana. Being conquered by Lord Rama's personality, I cannot be tempted with anything else in this world. Like sunlight is inseparable from the sun, Mother Sita is inseparable from

Lord Rama. Despite so many months of constant torment that you have subjected me to, I still give you a chance. Return me to Lord Rama now and I will ensure that you are not burnt by his wrath. If you want to save yourself and your illusory realm, this is the only chance.'

Ravana was furious with Sita's attitude. She hadn't budged an inch even after months of being in captivity. In sheer frustration, with the back of his hands, he hit two golden plates that contained the costly gifts he had got for her. The pandemonium created by the fall of the golden plates and their contents echoed in the valley of Ashok Vatika. Hanuman could see that Ravana's associates were trembling and their legs were quivering. Sita was as composed as ever. In fact, there was renewed strength in her resolve. She stared at him, challengingly. By this time, he had clenched his fist and was advancing towards her menacingly. Just in time, Mandodari rushed forward and stalled him by telling him that hitting a woman would show him in poor light in front of his subjects. Ravana, finding merit in her statement, stepped back, but warned Sita with heavy words. He said he would wait for a month more and if she didn't submit to his will, he would chop her up and eat her for breakfast.

With Ravana's exit, Ashok Vatika buzzed with whispers. The demonesses were whispering animatedly, amongst themselves, in small groups while looking at Sita in disgust. Sita shrank into her shell again. Gone was the strong persona that she had portrayed a few moments back. Hanuman realised that he had to approach her soon. There were two problems in doing that: one was—the demonesses guarding her wouldn't allow that to happen—the second one was more critical—Mother Sita wouldn't recognise him if he landed in front of her. She would even conclude that he was a henchman of Ravana in disguise. She could ignore him or worse, scream in panic, driving the guards of Ashok Vatika into action. He decided to wait patiently for the right opportunity.

As the sun set that day, Hanuman stealthily approached the tree under which Sita was seated. Being careful not to catch the attention of the guards or the demonesses, Hanuman managed to reach his destination and began to consider his strategy. By this time, the entire Ashok Vatika had come to a standstill and every member around that area was fast asleep. A few guards were pacing back and forth, patrolling the garden entrances. Just then, some movement below caught his attention. When Hanuman glanced below, he was shocked to see what Sita was doing. She had tied her long hair to a tree branch and was looping it around her neck in an attempt to end her life. He began to panic considering her predicament. He didn't want to act in haste. That could push Sita to give up immediately and strangulate herself, neither did he want to do something drastic that would make her scream in surprise and alert everyone.

As he silently prayed for wisdom, he had a brilliant idea on how to handle the situation. In a quiet, but clearly audible voice, he began to narrate the story of Lord Rama. In a poetic manner, he sang the story of Lord Rama right from his birth, banishment, exile in the forest to Sita's abduction. He described Lord Rama's efforts to find Sita and how Hanuman was now here with the message of her beloved. As soon as the narration began, Hanuman could see Sita slowly relaxing. By the time he ended, she had taken off the noose and was seated on the floor, below the tree, crying tears of joy. He now leaped and landed right in front of her, assuming a miniature form. Introducing himself as Lord Rama's servant, he enquired about her welfare.

Sita connected with the voice of Hanuman. When he landed in front of her, his appearance hadn't matter. All that mattered was that he was a well-wisher and a follower of Lord Rama. She became peaceful and was completely at ease in front of a total stranger, understanding well this person's intimate connection with Lord Rama. But, to be sure he was an emissary of Lord Rama, she decided to test Hanuman by asking him to describe Lord Rama's appearance in detail. With great joy, Hanuman began, 'Lord Rama's beauty is inexplicable. He has a beautiful greenish-golden complexion and his eyes resemble lotus petals. He has broad shoulders, mighty arms and a deep voice. He is reddish in four places: his eyes, his nails and palms, and the sole of his feet. He walks in four different gaits akin to a lion, a tiger, an elephant and a bull. He has eight elongated, shapely body parts: arms, fingers and toes, eyes, ears, nose, backbone and trunk. Ten appendages on Lord Rama's body represent a lotus: his skin, mouth, eyes, tongue, lips, palate, chest, nails, hands and feet.'

Realising that Mother Sita needed substantial proof to trust anyone in the magical, illusory kingdom of Lanka, Hanuman produced the signet ring that Lord Rama had given him. Holding the ring carefully between his palms, he extended his hands towards Mother Sita. Glancing at that ring brought a flood of tears in her eyes. Picking up the ring that had touched the delicate fingers of Lord Rama for so long, Sita became overwhelmed. Now, more than any other time in the last few months, she felt intense separation from her beloved. Lord Rama was so close to her now, yet so far. Sita kept glancing at the ring with love, crying and smiling at the same time. Occasionally, she would look at Hanuman with eyes filled with gratitude for this service.

If Hanuman had to place the ring in her hands, it would subtly indicate that he is superior to her. But, by allowing her to pick up the ring from his palms, he clearly indicated that he is inferior to her. Subtleness in behaviour is indicative of depth of sensitivity.

Hanuman instantly decided that he would end the misery of Mother Sita by taking her along with him to Lord Rama's shelter. He said, 'My dear Mother, kindly come with me. Sit on my back and I will take you to Lord Rama immediately. All your miseries will end in a few minutes.'

The words of Hanuman took Sita by surprise. Seeing her reaction, Hanuman understood the confusion in her mind. How could a tiny-sized monkey claim to carry her? Expanding himself into a giant size, he kneeled down with folded hands. Sita's jaw dropped when she saw that the tiny monkey had become much bigger than the tree she was sitting under. In the next instant, he again shrunk himself, resumed his normal size and stood in front of her, awaiting her decision. She made many excuses why she couldn't come along with him and he countered each one of them. Finally, she explained the real reason for her refusal and that impressed Hanuman. She explained that if she had to travel with him, the world would feel that her husband was incapable of saving her. A demon brought her to Lanka and a monkey brought her back. People would naturally ask, 'What role did the husband play in her rescue?' Realising that Mother Sita wanted the glory of her rescue to only go to her husband, Lord Rama, Hanuman decided to not pursue this matter.

Then Sita asked Hanuman the question that had been nagging her for the last few months. How was Rama? How was he faring without her? Hanuman understood Mother Sita's purpose of asking this question. He said, 'The beauty of Lord Rama that I had described to you was true but that was all before your abduction. From the time you have gone missing from his life, he has become emaciated due to his separation from you. In fact, Lord Rama has grown so thin now, that the signet ring I just gave you would fit his wrist like a bracelet.'

Sita felt united with Lord Rama in their shared pain of separation.

Interestingly, both Hanuman and Sita had evaluated each other before accepting the other as genuine. Though both were in a state of desperation, they did not take the risk of blindly believing the other.

The greatest blunders are made while celebrating proximity to success.

What is Your Real Size?

'Flying across the ocean is not an easy task. If you have managed it, you surely must be as powerful as Garuda or Vayu.' Sita was appreciating Hanuman for his monumental achievement. Having herself travelled on that path in the Pushpaka Vimana of Ravana and having seen the vastness of the ocean, she knew it was a formidable mission.

Immediately, Hanuman became uncomfortable. The last thing he expected his venerable Mother Sita to do was glorify him. Shifting the focus from himself, Hanuman began speaking, 'Let me assure you, O Divine Mother, in the entire monkey army there is not even one monkey who is less than me in abilities. All are either equal to me or better than me. Their wisdom is deep, their proficiency in wielding any sort of weapon is marvellous and their loyalty towards Lord Rama is impeccable.

'Lord Rama has picked me for this errand of delivering a message to you because he considers me the lowest in the cadre and fit as a messenger. Naturally, no King would want to risk their most competent men for such duties.'

Sita was impressed with Hanuman's humility. She said, 'Son, I have a doubt. Will you help me understand?'

When Hanuman heard the word *Son* from Mother Sita's mouth, he melted with joy. In fact, Hanuman had adopted a miniscule form only to inspire motherly affection in her, towards him. He nodded his head in excitement, eager to render his mother some service. She asked, 'I have seen you change sizes, so, I am confused; what is your real size?'

Hanuman became very happy with Mother Sita's enquiry. He humbly explained, 'I am always small. But, by God's grace, I can turn bigger in size when needed. God's power is great, therefore, I can grow big by taking shelter in Him. Otherwise, I am always small.'

Sita smiled with appreciation at the deeper meaning of Hanuman's innocent words. He continued speaking in the same humble tone of a messenger. He did not say he would protect Sita. He only declared emphatically, 'When I go back to Lord Rama and Lakshmana and tell them you are in Lanka, they along with Sugriva and his warriors are sure to rush to Lanka without wasting a moment. Please be patient and be assured that Lord Rama will come and take you back. I only request you to give me something that assures Lord Rama that I actually met the right person in Lanka.'

Sita removed a chudamani (headgear worn by married women) which she used to wear on her head. While handing it over to Hanuman, she told him to present it to her Lord Rama. 'Seeing this, he will remember three persons, since the jewel was given to me by my mother in the presence of Lord Rama and his father,' said Sita. She also narrated the story of the crow named Kakasura which had attacked her in Chitrakoot and how Lord Rama had saved her using a blade of grass, transforming it into a brahmastra (divine missile). This story wasn't known to anyone in the world except Lord Rama and her. Armed with these two gifts, Hanuman was ready to give her message to his eternal master.

Humility is a silent festival that is celebrated alone, but, appreciated by all.

Havoc in the Golden City

When they entered the garden, there was smoke everywhere. Everything was destroyed. Only ruins everywhere. The once celebrated royal gardens of Lanka, the pride of their King, were nothing but a crematorium now. The only tree that was still standing was the Ashoka tree under which Sita was still seated. But as they looked carefully, the destroyer wasn't visible. Commands were barked and soon, they spread out in ten directions to comb him out. Thinking that the culprit was hiding somewhere in fear, they approached Sita's tree. The only person alive in that area was Sita. The rest were either dead or had fled.

As soon as the leader of the 80,000 men that Ravana had deputed to look into the Ashok Vatika crisis approached Sita, something interesting happened. From the foliage of the tree, he could hear a crunching noise. He went closer to inspect properly. Suddenly, a half-eaten apple was smashed against his face. He was disgusted. He ordered one of his men to climb the tree to find out which animal was hiding up there. As soon as the man reached the upper part of the tree, a leg appeared that kicked him hard on his ribs. The man went flying and landed on the ground at a distance, vomiting blood. The man died on the spot.

Hearing the cry of the dying man, the entire army gathered to face their hidden enemy. Hanuman stepped out of the foliage and was now standing on a thick branch of the tree, with one hand on his hip and another holding a mace to his shoulder. Seeing Hanuman's strong physique, the soldiers gasped. Lunging forward, he jumped down and kicked two soldiers on their heads, cracking their skulls and killing them instantly. The leader gulped heavily and mustering some courage, ordered his men to attack. Instantly, thousands of soldiers began running towards Hanuman with raised weapons. Effortlessly swinging his mace wildly, Hanuman sent them back flying with all their limbs smashed. Every time he hit one of them, he would shout out with joy, 'Jai Shri Rama!'

Within minutes, all the 80,000 men were history and Hanuman continued eating fruits till the next batch arrived. This time, Ravana, not wanting to take a risk of deputing an incompetent leader, sent his own son, the heroic Akshay Kumar. A track record of not losing a single battle supported this hero's unflinching confidence. All that was shattered once Hanuman planted the first kick square on his chest. Hanuman hadn't even given him a chance to make the first move. Of course, he did try his best to overpower the wild monkey prince but nothing he did was even remotely effective. Finally, not wanting to prolong matters, Hanuman picked him up by his legs and spun him around several times before smashing him to the ground, crushing his head to pulp. The ghastly death of Akshay Kumar sent waves of panic in Lanka. Now, no one wanted to even come in the proximity of Hanuman.

An aggrieved Ravana was agitated at the loss of his dear son. With no other choice left, he assigned the task to Indrajit—his most powerful eldest son. Indrajit assessed the situation and understood that the enemy was not an ordinary one. Killing him was out of question. All he had to do was capture him by deceit. He used every illusory trick he knew during his attack on Hanuman. All his strategies failed to work on this divine monkey. Finally, he decided to use the most powerful and sure-shot weapon he had in his possession, the brahma pasha (divine infallible rope missile). Aiming the missile towards Hanuman's chest, Indrajit laughed. As soon as the missile of Lord Brahma hit Hanuman's chest, Hanuman froze. He considered his next move carefully. He concluded that his intention in destroying Ashok Vatika and Ravana's army wasn't to end everything on his very first visit. It was simply aimed at giving Ravana a powerful warning. Now that he had already caused sufficient damage and his reputation had been established in Lanka, it was time for a rendezvous with the King himself.

Concluding thus, he closed his eyes and allowed himself to be bound by the ropes of the brahma pasha. The soldiers who were observing this couldn't decipher the subtle smile on Hanuman's face when the ropes were binding him. Lord Brahma had blessed him that he wouldn't be affected by any weapons. But out of respect for the divine weapon and in order to meet Ravana, Hanuman allowed himself to be captured.

Seated on a high-raised golden throne, studded with emeralds, Ravana looked down upon the wily monkey that had brought Lanka to a standstill. He was disgusted with his army for their inability to capture this naughty and seemingly harmless monkey. Yet again, Hanuman, on seeing Ravana felt deep admiration for his personality. He was undoubtedly highly charismatic. If only he hadn't been an enemy of virtue, he could have been a world protector. But alas, all that was only wishful thinking! The reality was that this was a demon and that too the most vicious type. And Hanuman had a message for him—a message that would wake him up.

Since no one was offering him a seat, Hanuman thought it best to help himself. Coiling his tail behind his legs, Hanuman created a seat for himself. Purposefully, he raised the seat so high that it was clearly way above Ravana, such that Ravana had to now look up at him straining his neck. Hanuman introduced himself as the servant of Kaushalya's son, here, on the mission of finding Mother Sita. Hanuman warned Ravana to return Sita with dignity, failing which a disaster awaited him. Hearing such arrogant words from this monkey in his own court and in front of all his subordinates, Ravana screamed, 'Kill the monkey!'

As the guards rushed with raised weapons towards Hanuman, Vibhishana, the younger brother of Ravana stepped forward and dissuaded him from harming a mere messenger. He reminded the King of the code of conduct for warriors that strictly forbade harming a messenger. Hanuman was impressed at the audacity of this man to speak so boldly in front of Ravana. Considering merit in his brother's words, Ravana decided not to kill Hanuman but to do something worse.

Soon, hundreds of pieces of cloth were brought to the courtroom and wrapped around Hanuman's long tail. Everyone was amazed at the length the tail had assumed. When stretched completely, it almost covered the floor of the entire courtroom. Once the humongous project of tying cloth to the tail was completed, the cloth was set ablaze. As soon as the cloth caught fire, the tail came into action. So far, it had been lying motionless. Suddenly, it started moving around, rapidly flashing flames at the faces of people all around the courtroom. Ravana ordered that Hanuman be tied more firmly and taken out of the courtroom immediately. Once out of the palace, Hanuman was taken all over the city to demonstrate to the people of Lanka that their criminal had been caught and was being punished for his misdeeds. Ravana wanted to do this to calm the disturbed and fear-stricken minds of the Lankavasis. Of course, Hanuman used this as an opportunity to study Lanka's fortification. All around Lanka, peals of laughter were heard as Hanuman was being taken around. The people of Lanka were enjoying the monkey's suffering.

When Sita heard about the burning of Hanuman's tail, she offered an earnest prayer to the Fire God, requesting him not to hurt the tail. Suddenly, Hanuman couldn't feel any pain. He understood that it must be the result of Mother Sita's prayers. Immediately, he concluded that it was time for action now. He shrunk himself and slipped out of the ropes that had bound him. Only a piece of rope remained in the hands of the soldiers who were dragging him around. Looking around, they found him on the rooftop of a nearby building. They couldn't figure out how in the world he could reach there. As they looked at him in dismay, Hanuman, laughingly, set the entire building on fire with his tail. The soldiers rushed towards the building to capture Hanuman, but by that time, he had already jumped to the roof of another building and set that building on fire as well. Assuming a gigantic form, he jumped from one building to another, setting everything on fire. Except for Vibhishana's palace, soon, every other building was on fire. The golden city was burning!

From the top of the same mountain where he had stood before entering Lanka, he inspected the burning city. Screams of terror could be heard far in the distance. The dream city had now become a dreadful city.

As he laughed heartily at the plight of the Lankavasis, a sudden panic gripped him. Suddenly, his mood changed...

The best way to conquer an enemy is to conquer his confidence.

Rain in Lanka

This was absolutely nonsense. How could he have done this? Whose side was he on, after all? All the efforts had gone waste with this one foolish act of his. Hanuman was extremely upset with the new turn of events. Just when he was basking in the glory of his victory over Lanka, this happened. It began to rain.

The residents of Lanka started celebrating the onset of rains. There were shouts of joy everywhere. How could Indra, the God of Rains have done this? Was he on Lord Rama's side or Ravana's? Hanuman was upset with this development and decided to confront him. He spotted Indra way above in the clouds, planning to return having accomplished his task. Hanuman intercepted him and questioned his actions. Indra smiled and asked Hanuman to have a closer look at what was happening in Lanka.

Hanuman looked back and saw that everyone there was screaming in agony and had resumed running hither and thither. There was utter chaos in the city and the fire had raged even higher. But, what confused him the most was despite all that, it continued raining in Lanka. Hanuman turned to a smiling Indra in total confusion. Indra answered with a grin on his face, 'Hanuman, it's not raining water, but fuel.'

Hanuman became very happy with Indra's intelligence and returned to the mountaintop to watch the fun. As he was taking a bird's-eye view of Lanka, he saw that every nook and corner of the city had turned into an inferno. That's when panic gripped him yet again, but, this time, the reason was different. He had made the biggest blunder of his life. How could he have done this? If each and every corner of Lanka were up in flames, wouldn't Mother Sita be caught in the same fire too?

He began to curse himself as he sprinted towards Ashok Vatika. He had foolhardily destroyed the very reason for which he had come to Lanka in the first place. If Mother Sita was burnt in the fire, there would be no reason for him to live; he would throw himself in the fire too. How could he dare to face Sugriva, Lord Rama and Lakshmana now? This was the result of acting with excessive passion. Passion makes one blind to the realities of life and, then, one's actions are governed by one's obsessions. Anger had made him dumb and insensitive. An angry person is unsteady in his actions.

His mind was racing at a greater speed than his legs. The only difference was his legs were running in the present and his mind was racing in the future. His mind was analysing what would happen if Mother Sita actually perished in the fire created by him. If Mother Sita perished, Lord Rama and Lakshmana would also give up their bodies. Unable to forgive himself, so would Sugriva. On hearing this report, how would Bharata and Shatrughna survive? On learning that the most pious race of Ikshvaku has met its end, all beings would be tormented with grief and agony. I let my mind be dominated by anger and I am guilty of destroying the entire world, thought a visibly troubled Hanuman.

Just then, Hanuman reached Ashok Vatika. Suddenly, he began to see auspicious omens all around him. Somehow, on its own, his mind became peaceful, and positive thoughts began flowing in it again. How could fire harm fire? Mother Sita's purity was like the purity of fire itself. The power of her prayers had saved my tail from being burnt. How could she have perished in fire? She had been protected by her own chastity and the power of the holy names of Lord Rama, Hanuman ruminated.

At that moment, a celestial voice declared that Sita was absolutely safe and sound. Hanuman relaxed. He further verified about her safety in Ashok Vatika. Seeing her safe and secure, Hanuman was overjoyed. He sought her blessings and prepared to return to Lord Rama and the monkey army. If finding Mother Sita had been tough, getting Lord Rama here would be tougher. If coming alone had been difficult, returning with an army would be impossible. If managing one's own journey had been difficult, managing the journey of a thousand million monkeys would be madness...

The first letter of "anger" represents audacity and the last letter, repentance.

Found Sita I!

Every other search party had returned with news of failure. They reported how they had searched every nook and cranny of the area they had been assigned. But there was no news of Sita's whereabouts. Disappointed and dejected, they all returned to an even more grief-stricken Rama. Hope seemed to have eluded him. However, one person still did not give up hope—the person whom Lord Rama trusted the most in the monkey army.

Just then, there was pandemonium. From the southern direction, hordes of monkeys were returning, making a huge racket. Right amidst the army, flying above them was Hanuman. Lord Rama's eagerness and anxiety intensified on seeing the last phalanx of the monkey army return. He had no idea what news he would hear from them. Pressure mounted and they were still far away for Lord Rama to know exactly what news they had. Just then, he heard something he couldn't believe. As soon as he heard those words, Lord Rama was convinced that Hanuman was not just intelligent, but sensitive beyond comprehension. He had actually distorted the grammar of the language to give joy to Lord Rama.

At the top of his voice, Hanuman shouted, 'Found Sita I!'

As soon as he spotted Lord Rama, Hanuman realised his master must have been in under tremendous pressure without the knowledge of the outcome of the search operation. Seeing the leaders of all other search parties assembled around Lord Rama, Hanuman knew that his Lord was disappointed at their failure. He realised that he had to communicate properly to quell Lord Rama's anxiety. Analysing the situation, he knew he shouldn't say, 'I found Sita'. If he said the word *I* first, being surrounded by failures, Lord Rama might assume that *I* is going to be followed by, 'I did not find Sita'. Just the thought may cause His instant death. Hanuman also ruled out announcing, 'Sita I found', for even that would make Lord Rama arrive at the wrong conclusion.

The only word that would revive Lord Rama's hope and give Him the impetus to hold on till Hanuman reached Him was *found*. There was nectar filled in that one word. Though it was grammatically wrong, it was absolutely sensitive. Communication is not about perfection in grammar but about perfection in the ability to convey what a person wants to hear in a way that is sensitive and pleasing. By distorting grammar, Hanuman had given Lord Rama's morale a boost.

As soon as Hanuman and His team were near Lord Rama, they ran up to Him and conveyed that they had succeeded in finding Mother Sita in Lanka. Lord Rama enquired about the exact location and asked after Sita's welfare. Hanuman narrated each event in detail. His graphic description included everything that had taken place during his journey to Lanka and also within the island of Lanka. Finally, Hanuman brought out the chudamani given to him by Sita and handed it over to a teary-eyed Rama. Memories of His beloved came flooding back to Him and He couldn't be the sober, controlled leader anymore. He broke down and cried piteously. The entire monkey army assembled around the lord also wept seeing the plight of the person they loved so dearly. To lighten the mood, Hanuman narrated the episode of Kakasura that Mother Sita had shared with him. Seeing Sita's chudamani and hearing the story of Kakasura, Lord Rama knew beyond doubt that Hanuman had indeed met Sita. He got up and expressed His gratitude to Hanuman for having taken the trouble to find Sita. He told him that not just He, but the entire Raghu Dynasty was grateful for his heroic act.

Lord Rama continued speaking gracefully, 'O Hanuman, presently, I do not have anything valuable to offer you in appreciation of your tremendous service. For all that you have done for me, the only thing I have to offer is my loving embrace. Please accept it as my all.'

Lord Rama pulled Hanuman close to his heart and embraced him lovingly. In the embrace, Lord Hanuman literally melted. He closed his eyes and savoured every moment of that embrace. He wanted the memory of this embrace to remain in his subconscious memory forever. He was thinking how fortunate he was to receive this embrace that great sages hankered after, performing severe penances for thousands of years. Hanuman thought there was nothing more valuable than this that Lord Rama could have ever offered him. With that embrace, Hanuman got the inspiration to dedicate his life at Lord Rama's service and a desire to please Him in every possible way. He decided that his life's aspiration would be to receive another embrace from Lord Rama. And he knew exactly how that could happen...

Language is a medium of connecting hearts and not communicating words.

When the Impossible Became Possible

The impossible was done. In a matter of five days, the monkey army, under the guidance of architects Nala and Nila, worked together to construct an 100-yojana long and 10-yojana wide stone bridge across the ocean all the way till Lanka. The battle-eager army of Ravana waited with bated breath for the monkey army to arrive at their shores. Their hands were itching for a good fight. Little did they realise that this would be their last opportunity.

The fight between the two camps lasted indefinite hours over several days and nights. During the day, the monkey army had an upper hand, but the nocturnal demons exercised more power, using illusory tricks under the cover of night. The turning point in the battle was the entry of the trickster Indrajit, the son of Ravana. He launched all his attacks in an invisible mode. He moved at lightning speed, hurling weapons from different directions. None of the monkeys could decipher Indrajit's tricks, let alone attack him. Realising that the entire game plan depended on the brothers, Lord Rama and Lakshmana, Indrajit used a missile on them, given to him by Lord Brahma. The weapon successfully rendered Lakshmana unconscious.

With the fall of Lakshmana, the morale of the entire monkey army took a hit. Every monkey lost his purpose for fighting and they all dropped their weapons and ran to help the fallen hero. Meanwhile, the enemies began to slaughter the monkey army. There was panic in the monkey camp. Just then, Jambavan arrived at the scene. He had been fighting elsewhere and had thus taken time to reach there. The first question he asked was, 'Is Hanuman alive?'

Jambavan's confidence in Hanuman's ability was such that as long as he was alive, hope was alive. Hanuman made his way pushing through the crowd of monkey leaders and reached the centre where he saw Lakshmana lying unconscious. Tears ran down his cheeks. He was unable to accept that such a thing could happen to them. But seeing Jambavan unperturbed, he realised they still had a chance. He asked for the action plan. Jambavan promptly instructed Hanuman to bring four herbs that were available in the Himalayas. He explained the names of each herb and its medicinal properties. The first was named mrta-sanjivini that could restore a dead man to life. The second was called sailya-karani, used to extract embedded weapons and quickly heal wounds. The third was the suvarna-karni which was used to restore the body colour to its original texture. And finally, the fourth was the samdhani which was used to join fractured bones and severed limbs.

With the names entrenched in his mind, Hanuman headed towards the Himalayas. While Hanuman was away, Jambavan cleverly orchestrated a clean-up strategy in the battlefield where the monkeys were asked to dispose the bodies of all the demons into the ocean and collect the bodies of the dead monkeys together. The experienced Jambavan knew that as soon as the herbs were brought to the battlefield, something mystical would happen. He didn't want the benefit of their endeavour to be shared by the demons. Hence, the clean-up drive became mandatory. Once done, all they had to do was wait and pray for Hanuman's return—within the stipulated time—with the magic herbs.

Meanwhile, Hanuman had reached the majestic Himalayas after overcoming several challenges on his way. But the greatest challenge was identifying the herbs in the plethora of herbs that grew on these vast mountains. Being a novice in the field of medicine, he had no idea how to recognise them or distinguish one herb from the other. Had he had time, he could have surely figured it out, somehow. But today, time was ticking away much faster than ever, almost mocking his ability to match its speed. Unable to conclude which herb he had to pluck, Hanuman decided to do the impossible. He decided to carry the entire mountain back with him.

Uprooting the entire mountain, Hanuman flew back with great speed and determination. As soon as Hanuman came within the vicinity of the battlefield and the fragrance of the herbs entered Lakshmana's nostrils, he gained consciousness. Even the dead monkeys were revived by the power of the herbs. The celebration and euphoria in the monkey army was causing disgust and irritation in the rakshasa camp, more so because all their dead ones had been cleverly thrown into the ocean and couldn't be revived. Lord Rama felt relieved to see Lakshmana and embraced his brother. Hanuman returned the mountain to its original place and rejoined the last phase of the gruesome battle.

Soon, Lakshmana killed Indrajit and Hanuman exterminated the rest of the rakshasas. The final duel between Lord Rama and Ravana was watched with intense attention.

As torrents of arrows whizzed past in each direction, the monkey army was thrilled at their Lord's expertise. Though both were powerful, ultimately, Lord Rama released an arrow that penetrated through the navel of Ravana and sucked out his energy, leaving him lifeless. Vomiting blood from his ten heads, Ravana fell dead.

Cheers of joy broke out in the monkey army and they began to dance around Lord Rama and Laskhmana. All's well that ends well. It was time for a reunion...

Impossibility is a limitation set by a doubting mind. Encouragement expands its horizons.

The Great Story

Behind him, loud sounds of musical instruments and songs were audible. The monkey army was celebrating their victory and the rakshasa clan was celebrating their new King who promised a new era of justice and development. But Hanuman wasn't a part of this celebration; his mission was far from over. His happiness depended on Lord Rama's happiness. And, at this point in time, two worries preoccupied Lord Rama—reunion with Sita and reunion with Bharata.

As Hanuman walked towards Mother Sita, a constant thought on his mind was genuine appreciation for Lord Rama's sensitivity. Once the coronation of Vibhishana had taken place, Lord Rama instructed Hanuman to go to Ashok Vatika and bring Sita. As soon as he received the order from Lord Rama, Hanuman sprang to his feet and sprinted away. Just then, Lord Rama stopped Hanuman and called him back. Hanuman returned obediently and stood next to Lord Rama. Lord Rama told him, 'Vibhishana is the King of Lanka now; without his permission you should not venture into the inner sections of the city.' How sensitive Lord Rama was! No wonder, people were ready to offer their lives at His beck and call, thought Hanuman.

Spotting Hanuman enter the Ashok Vatika, the 700 demonesses who were guarding Sita stood up and parted way, allowing him to easily reach Sita. In each of their minds, the discomforting vision of his previous visit began to play out again. Knowing well that everything had changed in Lanka in the last seven days, the demonesses chose not to interfere with him. Noting the distinct change in their attitude, Hanuman walked towards Mother Sita, smiling. He informed her about the death of Ravana and the well-being of her beloved Rama. He happily announced that she was now free to return to her waiting husband. As promised, her husband had rescued her from this calamity. Tears of joy poured from Sita's eyes as blessings poured from her heart for Hanuman's assistance in her rescue.

As Sita prepared to leave, Hanuman stopped and asked her a question. He sought her permission to kill all the 700 demonesses who had harassed her during her 10-month stay in Lanka. He wanted to know how she preferred these people to be killed. Should he scratch them with his nails? Should he beat them with his fist? Should he smash them with his mace? Should he burn them with fire? Should he throw them into the ocean?

Sita smiled and answered, 'The mistake of a helpless servant is considered to be the mistake of his instructive master. These demonesses had no choice but to torture me. They didn't trouble me out of choice but out of compulsion. I wouldn't attribute the cause of my suffering to someone else, but, rather, accept it as a consequence my previous karmic action. In fact, the greatness of a person lies in his ability to forgive wrong action and not retaliate with another wrong action.

'Let me tell you a story which will help you understand this thought better.' Sita continued with a smile. 'Long back, there was a hunter in the forest, in search of his prey, when a tiger attacked him. Desperate to save his life, the hunter began to run at a frantic pace. Finally, finding himself unable to outsmart the tiger in the chase, he decided to climb a tree. On reaching the tree's top branch, he felt relieved to have been saved from the clutches of the tiger. That's when he noticed someone sitting next to him. In his desperation, he was blinded to the fact that on the same tree, there resided a huge bear. The bear had climbed up and settled down next to him on the same branch. The hunter trembled in fear, seeing a deadly beast stare at him from such a close distance. For a moment, he considered escaping by jumping down, but then he saw the open mouth of the tiger awaiting his arrival.

'He didn't know what to do. In great fear, he folded his hands and began to piteously beg the bear to be merciful to him. Surprisingly, the bear agreed and shifted a little further away from him. Seeing the reaction of the bear, the tiger standing below, signalled the bear to throw the man down. The bear flatly refused. The tiger tried to convince him by stating that human beings are common enemies of all animals in the jungle and that he shouldn't show mercy to these selfish beings. But the bear was an animal of strong principles. The tiger gave up and decided to wait under the tree. Meanwhile, the bear went to sleep while the hunter couldn't sleep a wink.

'After a couple of hours, the tiger signalled to the hunter to throw down the sleeping bear and promised not to harm him if he does so. The human considered merit in the tiger's words and decided to save his life by feeding the bear to the hungry tiger. With one hard shove, the man pushes the bear down the tree. But being very agile, the bear somehow caught hold of a lower branch of the tree and swung back to safety, avoiding the tiger. Once again, the hunter began to panic seeing the bear climb up towards him. The tiger ridiculed the bear's compassion for a selfish human being and urged him to throw him down immediately.

'The bear sat up on a branch and told the tiger that a virtuous soul does not give up good conduct, no matter how badly others treat him. Once a person has taken shelter, he should never be abandoned, no matter what happens. Why should he give up his goodness because of the hunter's badness?

'O Hanuman, if a bear can think in such an exalted manner, why can't we human beings learn to forgive the mistakes others commit? I forgive these demonesses who were innocent and were acting under the influence of Ravana.'

Tears gushed down Hanuman's cheeks when he heard the magnanimous thoughts of Mother Sita. Now he started analysing who was more sensitive between Lord Rama and Mother Sita. He quickly concluded that Mother Sita was definitely a million times more sensitive than Lord Rama for having shown sensitivity to those who harmed her.

Soon Sita was reunited with Lord Rama and both of them felt great ecstasy in being back together again. There was still a deadline that Lord Rama had to meet. Bharata had warned him that if he did not return on the day the 14-year exile got over, he would end his life. Lord Rama decided to borrow the Pushpaka Vimana—that was in Vibhishana's possession now—for his return to Ayodhya. Even though the aircraft could fly at the speed of thought, Lord Rama had to make several stops owing to his commitment to many sages. Somehow, he had to ensure that Bharata would delay his decision of jumping into the fire to end his life. He sent his disaster-management team ahead—the one person team...

The weak seek revenge. The strong offer forgiveness.

A Firefighter

As he stood in front of the burning pyre, he recalled everything that had transpired in the last 14 years. Something in his heart told him that his brother might never come back. He was an ascetic. Anyway, whatever it was, he had a vow to execute. So what if Lord Rama was attached to his vows and lifestyle, even he had the right to be attached to his own vow. He had very clearly told Lord Rama during their last meeting at Chitrakoot that he wouldn't wait a day more once 14 years of exile were completed. If Lord Rama delayed even by a day, he would end his life. Today was that day. A few minutes were left for the day to end and there was no sign of Lord Rama's return. He was ready to accept the unacceptable.

As the clock ticked away, Bharata grew more anxious. Shatrughna, his brother, all the ministers of Ayodhya and the prominent citizens had no idea how to prevent the determined Bharata from jumping into the fire. They could only pray that God would send some messenger to delay this fiery ordeal.

Above Bharata, on the branch of a tree sat Hanuman, wondering what to do. Lord Rama had sent him to inform

Bharata of his return but before he could do that, Bharata was already preparing to end his life. He recalled how a few weeks back, he was sitting on a tree like this, looking at Mother Sita contemplate suicide. And today, he saw Bharata do the same thing. Whenever he had come across dead ends in his adventures, he had used the same solution and it had always worked. When the monkeys were unable to decipher what to do at the ocean shore, they had narrated Rama Katha and Sampati had arrived to their rescue. When Mother Sita tried to end her life, he had again narrated Rama Katha, giving her hope to continue living. And today, as he watched the calamity unfold, he knew what to do.

Immediately, he began narrating the Rama Katha—from the beginning of Rama Lila till the point where Lord Rama had reached Bharadwaja Muni's ashram, while on his way to meet Bharata. When Bharata heard the sweet narration of his brother's pastimes, he abandoned the idea of ending his life. Hope had returned to Ayodhya and the messenger of hope had saved every member of Lord Rama's family from disaster. He had saved Mother Sita by bringing her the message of Lord Rama; he had saved Lord Rama by bringing him the news of Mother Sita's safety; he had saved Lakshmana by bringing the magical herbs from the Himalayas, and now, he had saved Bharata by bringing the news of Lord Rama's return.

Just as electric shocks are used by a doctor to revive a dying heart, similarly, inspiration is used by a well-wisher to revive dying hope.

The Real Diamond

A thanksgiving ceremony was organised after Lord Rama's coronation as the King of Ayodhya. However, a thought had been troubling the divine couple for many months now. So many people had served them with selflessness, but they hadn't been able to reciprocate adequately as they themselves had nothing in their possession to give away. Of course, they shared the love they had within their hearts, but now that they had resources, they wanted to offer more.

Each and every friend was called upon and duly honoured. Lord Rama made the announcement that though each one them was being awarded, the value of the gift was insignificant compared to the valuable service each of them had rendered in the past months. They chose to offer the last recognition to the most submissive and heroic personality who had, by now, become their favourite. When he was called, Hanuman walked up to the throne with his head cast downward as Lord Rama and Sita recollected tales of his heroism. Everyone in Ayodhya was spellbound by his achievements.

After the tales of Hanuman's valour were narrated, Lord Rama got up and embraced Hanuman telling the world that He could never repay sufficiently, His debt, to Hanuman. Sita declared that Hanuman deserved more honour than anyone else, and that she definitely wanted to offer a reward to the reluctant Hanuman. Hanuman reiterated that for him, an opportunity to be of service to Lord Rama was his greatest reward. Seeing Hanuman's hesitance to accept anything, Sita decided to offer him her own priceless bejewelled necklace. When Sita actually took off her invaluable necklace, people in the audience gasped. They praised Hanuman for receiving such an honour from the queen and considered him lucky.

Hanuman held out his hands and received the gift with absolute disinterest. He began to closely inspect the necklace from all angles. After twisting and turning it in all directions, Hanuman still couldn't see what he wanted to see. To the shock of all those present there, he then began to dismantle the necklace, tearing it to small shreds. He broke each and every diamond in the necklace and carefully reviewed its inner content. He began to smash the pieces of diamonds on the ground in disgust. Finally, after every part of the necklace was inspected and demolished, Hanuman looked up.

He found thousands of jaws dropped! None of the people in the audience could digest what had just happened. How could anyone destroy a royal gift? That too, right in front of the queen! When they saw that Hanuman wasn't even attempting to defend himself by justifying his actions, they became extremely upset and angry with him for his deplorable behaviour. All the prominent citizens of Ayodhya from different corners of the courtroom began to demand an explanation.

Hanuman humbly explained that he was breaking the stones to see if Mother Sita and Lord Rama were inside the necklace. For Hanuman, something was valuable only if it had the presence of the divine couple. And since the necklace and every diamond in that necklace were devoid of the couple's presence, the gift was useless for him. When Lord Rama and Sita heard this explanation, they were extremely pleased with Hanuman's devotion and smiled looking at each other. For them, he was their real diamond. But the others in the courtroom felt that their King and queen had been insulted by Hanuman's action. Some even began to joke about Hanuman's so-called devotion. They even said that his love for Lord Rama and Mother Sita was only a sham and had no real depth.

One of them challenged Hanuman, mockingly. He said, 'If you really don't value anything that doesn't have Lord Rama and Mother Sita in it, will you value your heart if it doesn't have Lord Rama and Mother Sita in it? How can you be sure that your heart has the divine couple inside it?'

Everyone burst out laughing, seeing the shrunken face of Hanuman. Amidst their laughter, everyone froze...

Hanuman now stood in the middle of the courtroom with his chest ripped open. Blood had spilled all over the courtroom. People were aghast at what he had done to himself. With his bare hands, he had ripped apart his chest. But what amazed everyone the most was, within his chest there was a beautiful image of Sita and Lord Rama enthroned within his heart. Lord Rama and Sita had tears in their eyes and the others had shame written on their faces. Everyone in the courtroom fell at the feet of their worshipable superhero and bhakta Hanuman.

Outer wealth cannot be bartered to acquire the gem of inner goodness.

The Permanent Resident

Every monkey came forward, paid his obeisance to Lord Rama and accepted a special gift from his hands and stepped back to his seat. Lord Rama had decided to greet every monkey in the army before the send-off. The previous day, the chiefs in the army had been felicitated. But Lord Rama felt that wasn't enough. He wanted to personally express his gratitude even to the lowest-ranking soldiers in the army as all of them had done more than what any family member would do. Once the felicitation ceremony was completed, he turned to the entire senior batch of monkeys and instructed them to return to their abodes and continue serving society according to the principles they had learnt under his guidance in the last few months.

Shedding tears of gratitude, all the monkeys departed from Ayodhya. Now, Lord Rama, Lakshmana and Hanuman were the only ones left. Lord Rama turned to Hanuman, and with tears in his eyes, asked him if he had any desire in his heart. Hanuman, for the first time, decided to express his desire to the Lord. He said, 'Please grant me the boon that my love for you remains forever. Let me not forget you even for a second. Let my attention be not diverted from your exclusive shelter and service. Let me not even aspire to serve anyone else in this world who is disconnected to you. Let me continue living till such time that your divine story is told and retold in this world. I do not seek anything else.'

Hearing Hanuman's words, filled with a sincere desire to serve him, Lord Rama became overwhelmed with emotions and while embracing him, shared his heart. He told him how he was indebted to Hanuman for each and every service he had rendered him. Yet again, Lord Rama reiterated that the only thing he could offer Hanuman for everything he had done and for everything he would be doing in the future was this embrace.

That moment, Hanuman took a major decision in his life; a decision people have not been able to comprehend even today. Hanuman felt that since the Lord had embraced his body several times now, he had acquired a special strength due to Lord Rama's mercy. Concluding thus, he decided that he would never go to the spiritual world. He would remain in the material world with this blessed body forever.

And of course, while living in this world, his idea was, wherever there would be a Rama Katha going on, he would go there, sit and carefully hear the narration while meditating on the glories of Lord Rama.

Even today, whenever and wherever Rama Lila is being discussed, there is Hanuman Lila going on somewhere…

A story remains alive through centuries when its message remains relevant to modern times.

Hanuman Folk Tales

Lord Rama's Pet

'A very good astrologer has come to Ayodhya today.' Word spread like wild fire in Ayodhya and hundreds of people flocked at different street junctures to consult this new astrologer. Reading horoscopes as well as the lines on palms was child's play for this astrologer. But, his goal was different. He was actually a thief in disguise who had come to steal something valuable. He advanced towards his goal cautiously. As soon as he reached his destination, he slowed down and relaxed. The royal palace of Ayodhya was his destination and he attempted to steal a glance at the royal treasure.

The astrologer in disguise was none other than Lord Shiva, who was desperate to steal a glance at Lord Rama—a child in the palace of Ayodhya. When Kaushalya, Lord Rama's mother, heard about the brilliance of this astrologer, she sent a request for an audience with him. He immediately agreed and made sure he didn't show any undue excitement. He was ushered respectfully into the royal threshold where Mother Kaushalya was eagerly waiting with her lovely son, Rama. His heart skipped a beat when Lord Shiva saw the Lord in such a lovable form. What happened next was something that disturbed Lord Shiva deeply. It was a total failure of his entire plan.

Mother Kaushalya gently nudged Lord Rama and the little child sweetly walked up to the divine astrologer, bent down gracefully and deftly touched his feet. Lord Shiva became numb! He was flabbergasted. He was embarrassed that Lord Rama had actually touched his feet. What transpired after that in Ayodhya, was all a haze. There was a great noise going on in his head. He could hear nothing of what people spoke to him nor could he focus on anything that happened there. Lord Shiva found it difficult to reconcile with what had happened.

A few hours later, as he walked out of the precincts of Ayodhya, he wondered how he could undo the event of that day in his life. That's when an interesting idea struck him. That very instant, he disappeared from Ayodhya in the north and appeared thousands of yojana away in Anjanadri, down south. Descending Mount Anjanadri, Lord Shiva contemplated his decision. The only way he could counteract the embarrassment he experienced at Lord Rama touching his feet was by rendering some menial service to him. And the only way Lord Rama would accept menial service as an act of repentance from Lord Shiva was if he served him through his partial incarnation. That's precisely why he had decided to come there. Here resided an expansion of Lord Shiva in the form of Hanuman.

It wasn't very difficult for him to convince the already eager Hanuman and his enthusiastic mother Anjana to take Hanuman with him to Ayodhya to visit Lord Rama. As Lord Shiva returned with Hanuman to Ayodhya, he devised a better plan this time—a plan that couldn't possibly lead to any further embarrassment.

Soon a monkey-trainer entered the land of Ayodhya with his very agile monkey who was dramatic and acrobatic. Hearing the drumbeats of the monkey-trainer, hundreds of citizens of Ayodhya flocked at the city square to watch the performance of the dynamic monkey, the likes of which they had never seen before. In sync with the drumbeats of the monkey-trainer, the monkey began his startling performance. The children of Ayodhya were spellbound as were the adults. After a short performance, the monkey-trainer and his monkey walked away to perform elsewhere. The entire crowd followed, mesmerised. They were unable to take their eyes off the two. Both of them attracted the audience like a magnet.

People were discussing that this monkey-trainer was such an expert in playing the drums that he seemed almost as competent as Lord Shiva himself. The children of Ayodhya were all over the two and constantly trying to get the attention of the darling monkey. Soon, the crowd reached the royal palace. Situating themselves in a strategic spot, the trainer began playing his drum and the monkey began dancing. Their gaze was fixed at the palace gateway.

By now, a bigger crowd had thronged to watch the performance. The monkey and his master were unconcerned about who or how many were watching them. They were waiting for someone special. Finally, the breathtaking moment arrived when Lord Rama came running out of the palace along with his three brothers. King Dasharatha and his three prominent queens tagged along at a little distance. Both the monkey and his trainer skipped a heartbeat when they saw Lord Rama for the first time. In their effort to impress Lord Rama, the two performed with renewed energy. The drummer began to drum in a way that was humanly impossible. The rhythms from his drum mesmerised all the spectators. One couldn't help but dance. The monkey somersaulted, jumped, danced, spun, and hopped, all at the speed of the mind. Lord Rama was jumping and clapping with joy. Lord Rama's reaction excited the two further and they performed even better. The whole scenario reached a feverish pitch and finally the monkey-trainer pair slowed down and brought their performance to a halt. People around clapped, whistled, showered praises and offered gold coins to them. The King himself came forward to reward the performance.

Just then, Lord Rama said something stunning. With a sweet voice he said, 'Father, I want to keep this monkey for myself.'

King Dasharatha was quite embarrassed by this childish request. But the monkey-trainer and his monkey were visibly thrilled. The trainer lifted the monkey in his hands and gently placed him in the loving arms of Lord Rama. As the monkey landed in Lord Rama's arms, he closed his eyes to savour the experience of the first touch of his master. The divine touch thrilled him and every hair on his body stood in ecstasy. There were tears of joy in his eyes as Lord Rama embraced him tightly to his bosom. He had reached his destination.

Everyone's eyes were riveted to the unique scene of their beloved Rama holding a monkey so dearly. King Dasharatha wanted to reward the monkey-trainer for selflessly giving away his monkey. As he turned to look at him, he couldn't find him. He looked around. All the citizens tried to locate him. It seemed that he had disappeared into thin air. Was it so? Not really, for he remained in Ayodhya in the form of his expansion—the divine monkey.

Lord Rama was so happy to receive his pet monkey that he played with the monkey all day and all night. The monkey too was overjoyed being with his eternal master and he tagged along with Lord Rama and ran small errands for him. And when there was nothing else to do, he would just stare at him. Years passed. The monkey became a part of Lord Rama's life. He was with him when he learnt martial arts, when he played with his brothers, when he rode horses and he even slept in the same room, under Lord Rama's bed. And first thing in the morning, Lord Rama would pick him up and embrace him. In fact, many nights the monkey wouldn't sleep in anticipation of the loving embrace in the morning.

One day, Lord Rama wanted to fly a kite along with his brothers on the terrace of the palace. The monkey held the kite and released it when instructed. The kite began to soar in the sky with the expert handling of the thread by Lord Rama. The kite flew so high that it disappeared into the clouds. The boys couldn't see it anymore. Lord Rama released more thread and the kite soared higher and higher. At some point, the kite got stuck. No matter how much Lord Rama tugged at the thread, he just couldn't release it. He instructed the monkey to climb the thread and reach up to the kite and release it.

Skilfully, the monkey jumped up onto the thread and nimbly climbed up. He went higher and higher and soon disappeared into the clouds himself. As he climbed even further, he realised that the kite had reached the heavens. When he reached there, he saw Jayanta, Indra's son holding the kite and not allowing it to fly any further or return. He requested Jayanta to release it since it belonged to Lord Rama. Jayanta refused. The monkey assumed its original form of

Hanuman and assured Jayanta that Lord Rama would meet him in Chitrakoot. Once assured, Jayanta let go of the kite and Hanuman resumed the form of the playful monkey and returned to his Master, soaring on the kite. When the boys saw the pet monkey fly, balancing on the kite, they were thrilled and began to laugh and clap their hands.

The good days for the monkey came to an end rather abruptly one day. This was the day Sage Vishwamitra walked into Ayodhya. He requested King Dasharatha to hand over Lord Rama to him. After much argument, King Dasharatha agreed to part with his son. On hearing the verdict of his father, Lord Rama returned to his room and spoke to his pet monkey. He said, 'Hanuman, our time together has come to an end, temporarily though. I need to embark on my life's mission. You leave Ayodhya and join Sugriva as his minister. One day, I will come there and you shall reunite with me and be an eternal part of my mission thereon.'

The careless joys of childhood were replaced by responsibilities of adulthood. With responsibility comes sacrifice. Lord Rama first sacrificed his association with Hanuman and Hanuman sacrificed his freedom by serving Sugriva according to the instruction of Lord Rama.

When good times end, time for responsibility begins.

A Stone-melting Musical Tale

'Monkeys do learn music! Don't you know our hero Hanuman is an expert in music?' A monkey mother was trying to inspire her restless son to spend some time learning soft skills. The child was only interested in fighting and martial arts. As soon as the mother took Hanuman's name, his ears stood up. He dropped his mace and came running to her to hear more.

Her son's eagerness prompted the mother to narrate a little-known story from Hanuman's life. She believed that such incidents from the life of great heroes ought to be preserved for posterity to introspect on the multifaceted talents of the heroes of the past. The monkey boy sat cross-legged in front of her with eyes wide open and his hands holding his face with elbows resting on his legs. He was excited and wanted to devour this new story of his hero.

'One day, Hanuman heard a veena being played and its melody kindled his passion for music. Instantly, he decided to master every facet of music and learn to play all musical instruments. Getting up, he ran towards the direction from where the sound was emanating and found the saintly Narada playing his famous veena, absorbed in his love for the

Supreme Lord. Hanuman fell at his feet and clutched them, not ready to leave till he agreed to impart music lessons.

Within a few days, Hanuman mastered every aspect of music and could play every instrument in incredible styles. He had become a maestro in an unbelievably short duration. After the training, Narada wanted to examine his disciple. He requested Hanuman to sing a very complicated melody. Preparing himself to clear the examination, Hanuman sat on the ground in the lotus posture and closed his eyes. After clearing his throat, he began to sing in a melodious voice. His soul-stirring singing mesmerised Narada to such an extent that he became numb. He could do nothing but close his eyes and sway. He felt goose bumps on every inch of his divine body. He lost his grip on the veena and he didn't even realise it.

Hanuman's singing was so intense that the entire surrounding melted in ecstasy. Every rocky stone in the area melted. Flowers rained from trees, celebrating the joy of creation. Animals and birds sat around with closed eyes, absorbed in the divine song. Oblivious to the world, Hanuman continued singing with great joy in his heart.

After what seemed to be a really short time, Hanuman ended his soul-stirring song. As soon as Hanuman stopped singing, everything returned to its natural state. Birds and animals shook themselves out of their reverie and started moving away. Rocks regained their original state. Narada fumbled with words to glorify his prodigy disciple. Just then, he realised that his veena had fallen off his hands. He bent down to pick it up before walking up to congratulate his disciple. Being lightweight, the veena was not a burden for him to carry and, naturally, he put in minimum effort to pick it up with one hand.

It didn't budge. It was stuck to the ground. Try as he may, but he couldn't pull it off. The veena had fallen on a rock that had melted during Hanuman's performance. After he had stopped singing, the rock had resumed its natural hardness and the veena was now embedded in it. By now, Narada was sweating. He even tried singing to get the rock to melt again. All in vain.

Realising he needed help, he turned towards Hanuman who was, by now, grinning naughtily. Pointing at the stuck veena, Narada signalled him to help. Hanuman started stepping back. Seeing him step back, Narada stepped towards him. Soon, Hanuman turned around and started walking away. Narada was dismayed; he began to walk after him. Hanuman increased his pace and so did Narada. Soon, Hanuman was running furiously and Narada pursuing him in a hot chase. The two of them were chasing each other throughout the entire region, crossing mountains, running through dense forests and jumping over rocks and bushes.

Finally, after running through every nook and cranny of that region, Hanuman came back to the original spot, next to the veena, and sat down peacefully. Narada followed and flopped down next to him. He just couldn't understand why they had run like madmen. After catching his breath, he looked at Hanuman who seemed completely relaxed.

'Why did you run away like that?' Narada asked, visibly irritated and disturbed.

With folded hands and a very humble demeanour, Hanuman said something that touched Narada's heart. 'My dear Master, I wanted the dust of your lotus feet to sanctify each and every corner of this area. There was no other way this could have happened except through this trick. Please forgive me for making you run like this.'

Having said that, Hanuman began singing again and in a few seconds, the rock melted. Narada could easily pluck out his veena. Narada was impressed not only by his disciple's skill but also by his veneration for the potency of the spiritual master's dust. Blessing him that his singing would always attract the Lord's attention, he proceeded in search of other qualified and uniquely interesting disciples like Hanuman.

When you marry skills, success is born. But when you marry good attitudes, gratitude is born.

A successful person looks for limelight. A grateful person looks for the person who pushed him into limelight.

The Liquor Lake

What a scene!

Have you ever heard of a lake of liquor? Even if you have, have you ever heard of someone swimming in it, or someone sleeping in it? That was the scene the Lankan soldiers witnessed upon reaching there.

Floating on the lake of liquor was the mighty son of Prahasta, named Jambumali. They were totally flabbergasted to see him so casually floating in the liquor lake in his slumber. Occasionally, he would wake up, dip a glass into the lake, drink it and immerse himself into the liquor lake. He was so enthusiastic about drinking that he didn't even have the patience to wait for the drink to be brought to him; instead, he chose to stay immersed in the drink itself. They had seen many drunkards in Lanka, but this was indeed the King of all.

Of course there was a second hidden reason why Ravana had created this lake of liquor for Jambumali. When awake, he was an extremely restless and a powerful demon that couldn't be easily controlled. He needed to be kept occupied all the time; else, he would pick fights and beat up his own people.

As the soldiers stared at him, they were conscious of the fact that they couldn't continue admiring him for too long. There was an emergency in Lanka and they had been given the task of fetching Jambumali to deal with it. One soldier swam up to the floating demon and quietly filled his glass with anti-liquor medicine and returned to the shore. They waited patiently for him to get up for his next dose of liquor. He woke up sooner than expected and unwittingly drank the contents of his glass. In a few seconds, the anti-liquor medicine began to stir up his insides and he woke up abruptly. He began to thrash around violently, knowing full well that he had been tricked. He swam towards the shore and he was furious with the troupe of Lankan soldiers. Though the soldiers were trembling with fear, they decided to speak bravely.

Before he began to beat them up, one of the soldiers managed to narrate the emergency in Lanka. 'The King is anxious.' This piece of information was enough to stop him in his tracks and think. He realised that the situation was graver than he had expected. He moved at a quick pace to Ravana's courtroom.

'Why have you brought me down from paradise? It had better be a good reason.' Jambumali's voice, though arrogant, was extremely powerful. Ravana hated the tone with which he spoke, but there was no option but to tolerate. He was aware of Jambumali's power. There were times when nothing else and no one else worked like him. This was one such time.

'There is a tough fight waiting for you!' Ravana said.

'Whom do you want me to fight against this time? Is it Indra or Agni?' Jambumali was excited at the proposal of a good fight.

'A monkey!' Ravana said with concern in his voice.

'What nonsense! I am going back to sleep. Send one of your tiny soldiers to deal with a nuisance monkey. I am going back.'

'The Ashok Vatika has been destroyed.' There was not just concern but great helplessness on Ravana's face as the mighty King spoke about his favourite and heavily secured garden being demolished. 'He is not an ordinary monkey. He has already destroyed hundreds of our soldiers. He has to be stopped now.'

Jambumali stopped in his tracks and agreed to take on the task. Ravana sent along with him 80,000 soldiers to assist him. Initially, Jambumali felt that he didn't need any assistance and that it was below his dignity to accept help. But, on Ravana's insistence, he reluctantly agreed.

When the army reached the borders of Ashok Vatika, they saw something amazing. On the topmost dome of a palace sat a colossal monkey, munching away on fruits. On spotting the approaching army, Hanuman stood up with his hands on his hips and said. 'Who wants to die today? I am the servant of Lord Rama; who has the guts to challenge me?'

Jambumali yelled back, 'You foolish monkey! Don't you know where you are standing? You are in the abode of the mighty Ravana. The demigods are cutting vegetables in the kitchen. The Nava Grahas (nine planets) that decide ordinary people's destiny are fated to serve Ravana as footholds to his throne. My father, Prahasta, eats giant mountains and digests them like peanuts.'

Hanuman took his words very lightly, 'All that was in the past. The present is ME. Look at the state of Lanka. I have destroyed all your beautiful gardens.'

Jambumali was so furious with Hanuman's words that he began to shoot arrows at him. Hanuman jumped off the palace and landed next to a tree. He uprooted it and hurled it towards the demon. Soon, a volley of rocks and trees followed. Jambumali shot down the rustic weapons deftly with his sharp arrows. He followed it up by attacking Hanuman with deadly missiles. Hanuman laughed at his useless shower of arrows. He caught the missiles and flung them back on his army and some he simply deflected with a slap as they turned around and rained on the Lankan soldiers.

When Jambumali realised that his weapons were useless in front of Hanuman, he decided to resort to magic. He closed his eyes and grew in size. He grew so big that Hanuman was only up to his knees. With renewed confidence that he could now crush the monkey, Jambumali opened his eyes. All he could see was a couple of rounded walls right in front of his eyes. What was that? He had never seen anything like this. He was so confused that he began to look all around. Suddenly, he heard a booming voice high above him. He strained his neck up. He was shocked!

Hanuman was staring down at him. The round objects that reached his eye level were Hanuman's knees. Even though he had grown big, Hanuman had grown much bigger than he could have imagined. He couldn't grow any bigger now.

He realised that his individual power was failing in front of Hanuman. He decided to rally the collective power of 80,000 soldiers at once. He looked back to direct his army. Another surprise awaited him! Where was his army? A huge mountain was standing in the place where Ravana's army had been stationed earlier. It was clear that Hanuman had not just grown to a massive height in these few minutes, but, he had also lifted an entire mountain and smashed all the 80,000 soldiers under its weight in a flash. Everything had happened so quickly that it seemed the army had not had any opportunity to react and save their lives.

Hanuman mocked at the shocked demon, 'My dear Jambu, what will you do now? Will you take shelter at my feet?'

'All this is an illusion! If you have the guts, come back to your original form and face me. I shall also assume my original size.'

Both returned to their regular size and faced each other. Hanuman began to walk around Jambumali who had to keep whirling around to face him. He said, 'Jambu, these are the last three minutes of your life. I have a pious suggestion for you. I can teach you a special mantra which is very small and very easy. It's just two syllables. This mantra will completely undo all the sins that you have committed in this lifetime and many more. Not only that, if you chant this mantra while dying, you shall reach the highest destination possible. Chant after me, Ra-ma. Ra-ma.'

Jambumali was quite surprised at the turn of events. He said, 'What nonsense is this? I have not come to learn mantras from a monkey! I have come to kill you.'

Hanuman was too casual about the whole thing, 'That you cannot do, anyway; might as well learn this mantra.'

This was too much for Jambumali's ego. No one had ever taken him so lightly. He rushed towards Hanuman and jumped on him. Hanuman dug his index finger into his navel; and effortlessly picked him up with just one finger. He lifted him all the way up, above his head and spun him around on his single finger. After spinning him forcefully at high speed, Hanuman flung him aside, pushing all his internal organs out through his mouth, leading to a miserable death.

'R..A..M..A!   R..A..M..A!   R..A..M..A!' Hanuman continued chanting and walked away.

For a vain student, facing up to a mistake feels like bearing down on the ego.

The Greatest Blessing

Today was a day of action. With one call of Sugriva, millions of monkeys from the world over had assembled. The task had been clearly explained to them. Find Sita! No one had any idea where she could be. Except that she was kidnapped and some animals had indicated that it could be the southern direction. But that didn't mean anything. A flying machine could be manoeuvred in any direction. Venturing south could have easily been a ploy to fool the chance observers.

There was an air of excitement across the ranks of the monkey army. Not only because they were to be a part of something interesting, but more so because this was an opportunity to serve someone as illustrious as Lord Rama, the Sun Prince. Even within such a short span of time, each monkey in the army had developed immense love and appreciation for him.

When they were told that Lord Rama would individually meet them before venturing out, their excitement knew no bounds. Probably, for the first time in their lives, the monkeys were receiving so much respect and trust from the human society. Moreover, this was not just anyone in the human society, but the most respectable soul. They were clearly grateful.

They lined up to meet Lord Rama. Each monkey got to be in the presence of Lord Rama for a few seconds and receive his blessings and grace. Though it was for a very short period, it was a very fulfilling experience for the monkeys. At the end of the long winding line, Hanuman was standing meekly. Time and again, Lord Rama's eyes were searching out for him.

Finally, when Hanuman's turn came, Lord Rama was very happy but at the same time he wanted to test his dear servant. 'Where have you been all this while? I have been waiting to see you.'

Hanuman rushed forward and bent low holding Lord Rama's feet. Lord Rama in turn bent down and touched his shoulders to lift him up. Staying in the bent, respectful position of holding his feet, Hanuman spoke, 'My Lord, please allow me to remain in this position. As long as I cling to your feet, there is hope for me. The moment you lift me, you will leave me. As long as I am bowing at your feet, your hands will remain on my shoulders. This is the safest position for a living entity. On the one hand, I have the fortune of holding your feet and on the other hand, I am being held by your able arms. Hope and assurance are both available to me in this position.'

Lord Rama was impressed but he was still interested in testing Hanuman's wit. He said, 'My dear Hanuman, all that is fine. But since you have come so late, I have nothing to offer you now. All my blessings are exhausted. What can I offer you now?'

With a twinkle in his eyes, Hanuman replied, 'My Master, you may have given all the big things in your possession. You have given away knowledge of the scriptures, your wisdom and guidance, power, fame, and more. But frankly, I am not looking for those big things. I am interested in the smallest thing that you have. If you could gift me only that, I would consider myself the most fortunate.'

Lord Rama was intrigued by this request. What did he have which he hadn't yet given away? Moreover, what was the smallest thing in his possession? Reading confusion on Lord Rama's face, Hanuman smiled.

'My Lord, you yourself had told Lord Parashurama that the smallest thing in your possession is your name—Rama. Please give me your *small* name.' Hanuman was delighted as he spoke these words. He continued, 'Though your name is the smallest possession you have, still it contains the entire brahmanda (universe).'

Lord Rama was thrilled with Hanuman's explanation and impressed by his profound wisdom in winning hearts. With tears in his eyes, Lord Rama embraced Hanuman.

There was nothing to be spoken. Hanuman had said it all.

From then on, Lord Rama's name was owned by one person—Hanuman!

Just like the smallest seeds may contain the biggest trees, the smallest truths contain the greatest secrets.

Puzzle of the Floating Stones

There was sadness in the monkey army today. All the leaders, despite putting their brains together, couldn't figure out a solution to this serious problem. Even Nala and Nila—the best minds—couldn't fathom a working solution with their expertise. On his part, Lord Rama seemed least interested in helping them because he trusted their intelligence and capabilities. This added to the army's responsibility. After a whole day of thinking, they were exhausted and utterly frustrated.

Hanuman, in particular, was feeling most helpless since this problem didn't even concern him. Why would he worry about how to cross the ocean when he had recently flown to Lanka and returned? Yet, the question remained. How would the huge monkey army cross the ocean? Hanuman sometimes wondered why Lord Rama needed such a huge army when he himself could destroy Lanka and bring back Mother Sita. But he never had the courage to ask Lord Rama this question because he knew that his Lord strongly believed in encouraging everyone to work together to achieve a goal.

Anyway, this wasn't the time to argue, but to find a tangible solution. Thousands of monkeys stood along the seashore, staring blankly at the massive stretch of water that lay ahead of them. Many of them were crying tears of helplessness. All of them had done so much in finding Sita's whereabouts. The entire globe had been scanned in a little over a month. And now, though they knew where she was, they couldn't get there. Hanuman could clearly read all their minds and knew he had to solve their problem.

But he was equally helpless. During such despondent times, he had the habit of loudly chanting Lord Rama's name, seeking the Lord's guidance to bestow intelligence on him. In utter frustration, he threw a stone into the water as if to admonish the ocean for not giving way.

Unbelievable!

How could this happen? Hanuman was overjoyed and was jumping in the air. Seeing Hanuman's excitement, the monkey army gathered around him. He showed them how the stone he had thrown into the water was comfortably floating. He took another stone and threw it. Drowned! He threw more and more stones and invariably every stone sank. But the first stone that he'd thrown was floating. It inspired the monkey leaders with a new possibility. All of them joined Hanuman to decode the secret of the floating stone. They began throwing stones of various sizes, shapes and weights in order to ascertain what was responsible for that stone to float.

Hanuman realised that throwing stones mechanically wouldn't help. He contemplated what exactly he was doing when he threw that stone. That's when he realised what the additional unascertained factor was—Lord Rama's name!

To test his conclusion, Hanuman threw another stone taking Lord Rama's name. Lo and behold, it floated! There was euphoria in the monkey camp. All the monkeys were jumping, whooping and clapping their hands at this novel discovery. Each one began to toss stones into the water, taking Lord Rama's name and, invariably, every stone floated. They had found their solution! All they had to do now was pool in enough stones to construct a stone bridge across the ocean.

The work began. Most monkeys were extremely busy in procuring sizeable stones from far and wide, while some supervised the construction of the bridge and organised the placement of the stones. Lord Rama was impressed with the efficiency of the monkeys and was eager to assist in some way. What intrigued Him the most was the puzzle of the floating stones. No one really wanted to embarrass Him by telling Him that they were taking His name and the power of His name made the stones float. Though Lord Rama saw the monkeys throw the stones taking His name, He didn't really want to connect the two due to His humility. Nonetheless, Lord Rama wanted to help with the construction of the bridge. Not wanting to be in the limelight, Lord Rama chose a quiet corner to make His contribution to the construction project.

Taking a sizeable boulder, He threw it into the ocean. To His utter disappointment, the stone sank. He picked up another stone and this time threw it into the ocean taking His own name, following the trend. To His greater dismay, the stone sank yet again. He was totally confused now and, in fact, became a bit embarrassed at His non-performance. Just then, a gentle voice startled Him.

Hanuman was kneeling on one leg, with his other leg stationed on the ground. His head was bent down and eyes closed. With folded hands he said, 'My Lord, how do You expect the stone to float? Anyone or anything that

You have rejected and thrown away is meant to drown. There is no hope for the rejected. When You decide to give up on someone, there is no possibility of liberation from the ocean of material existence for that person. However, when we throw the stones taking Your holy name, the stones float with the hope that they can be of service to You and receive the grace of Your lotus feet. So kindly allow us to utilise these stones in Your service. Please don't reject them and deny them an opportunity to serve You.'

Seeing logic in Hanuman's proposition, Lord Rama walked away from the bridge-building exercise, understanding that some tasks are best left to His name...

Trying to generate an idea is like trying to generate rain. Catch it when it comes.

Mountainous Devotion

The southern part of the land was covered. Every major mountain, hill and rocky terrain had been explored. The construction of a 100-yojana long and 10-yojana wide stone bridge wasn't that easy. There was acute shortage of stones now. Only Hanuman could venture far north to procure huge stones available in abundance there. Thus began Hanuman's frequent north-south trips, traversing the landmass several times a day.

After innumerable trips, he was tired of flying in and out. In addition, the flying time itself was too much. He decided that enough was enough. This trip, he wasn't going to get big boulders, he would just pluck out an entire hill. Already, the bridge project was in its last phase. If he just managed to get a mountain big enough, there wouldn't be any need for the other monkeys to take more trouble. With this in mind, he ventured far north to the Himalayas.

After scanning for a considerable period of time, he found just the thing he was looking for. It was the most magnificent hill he had ever seen. All his life, he had spent on different hills and mountains. Most of them had very similar terrains. But this one was way different. It almost seemed out of this world. The natural beauty was exquisite. There were beautiful lakes on it; even the trees seemed to be from the spiritual realms. As soon as Hanuman set his eyes on it, the hill started throbbing. It began bouncing, as if, expressing its eagerness to travel with Hanuman.

Plucking out the entire hill, Hanuman carried it on his palm and took off. As he was flying southwards, a monkey sent by Nila, the Chief Architect of the bridge project intercepted him. The bridge was completed. No more rocks were needed. Hanuman was required to report back. Hearing the instruction, Hanuman began his descent immediately to place the hill on the land above which he was hovering. A few drops of water began to wet Hanuman. Interestingly, they were hot unlike cold raindrops.

Completing his descent, he placed the mighty hill below and observed it. That's when he realised that the hill had been shedding tears and seemed very disturbed. Addressing the mountain, he said, 'You seem to be a special hill with emotions and love in your heart. May I know who you are and why you are shedding tears?'

The hill thundered, 'I am Govardhan, the King of Hills. I was eagerly waiting for an opportunity to serve Lord Rama. I have been sent to this world only to assist in the Lord's pastimes. I looked forward to fulfilling my life's mission and suddenly I realise the Lord doesn't need my service anymore. I am totally disgusted with myself. How can I live after knowing that the Lord doesn't need me anymore?'

Hanuman was so touched by Govardhan's devotion that he decided to personally appeal to the Lord. Reassuring the hill about the Lord's love for his devotees and his own sympathy at this situation, Hanuman flew back to the scene of the bridge building. By the time he reached, the bridge was complete and the monkey army was packing up to begin their siege of Lanka. Finding Lord Rama alone in one corner of the ocean longingly looking towards Lanka where his beloved was captive, Hanuman approached him in all humility.

Hanuman narrated his unique experience with this hill named Govardhan. He praised Govardhan's devotion profusely and requested the Lord to consider this hill as a special case to bestow his mercy upon. On hearing the eagerness of the hill to serve him, Lord Rama told Hanuman that in his next incarnation as Krishna, he would bestow his blessings to this hill for its devotion. In fact, Lord Rama told Hanuman that he would spend most of his 11 years of stay in Vrindavan on the Govardhan Hill. Not just that, since Govardhan had such sincerity and a personal touch with the Lord, as Krishna, he would carry the hill on his finger for 7 days and 7 nights continuously.

A happy Hanuman conveyed Lord Rama's message to a happier Govardhan. Only a person who loves to serve can understand the joy of a person who has been assured unlimited service.

Eagerness feeds hope like air feeds fire.

The Bhasmalochana Scare

Perhaps, this was the most difficult time during the war. No one knew how to deal with this calamity. No weapons, no army involved. Just one man!

He was walking all over the battlefield, creating madness. Whichever direction he looked, there were heaps of ashes. They had all heard of him, but no one knew him. Not even Vibhishana. He had just come from the netherworld, Patalaloka. Ravana had been there on the pretext of visiting Bali, the saintly King of the Demons. But little did the monkey army realise that he never accomplished only one task with any visit. He had definitely invited this terrible demon with a fiery vision, named Bhasmalochana.

With the death of his brother Kumbhakarna, Ravana had gone mad with rage. He was killing his own people to overcome his frustration. That was till he got the brilliant idea of calling Bhasmalochana to lead the army and launch an attack. The next day, when the monkey army became aware that a nondescript was becoming the commander of the Lankan army, there was jubilation amongst them. They were overconfident that because Ravana had lost all his important generals, he was now forced to appoint demon as chief of the army.

They were at their wits' end when they saw only one person walking out from the Lankan doorway, that day. Something was wrong here! Something terribly wrong! This man walked out confidently towards the waiting monkey army. What was most surprising was that he was not just alone, but alone and blindfolded!

Initially, the monkeys giggled, but as the man came closer, the leather band he was wearing over his eyes became more and more visible. There was clearly a glow underneath the band. His eyes were glowing! That's when realisation dawned on the monkeys. Bhasmalochana! The man who could burn with his vision!

Panic struck the whole monkey army. The monkeys began to run helter-skelter. No one wanted to be around when this man removed his blindfold. Literally trampling each other, the monkey army began to retreat. The leaders of the army were confused. They had no idea what to expect. Yes, they had understood the obvious. But what they didn't understand was the unobvious. There was only one question on everyone's mind, the most obvious one, 'What to do now?'

Just then, the inevitable happened. Bhasmalochana removed his blindfold. His eyes were shining like the noonday sun. Whichever direction he glanced, there was a flash of light, a short scream, the smell of flesh burning and a heap of ashes. Soon, across the battlefield, there was burning of live bodies. The bodies did not take even a few seconds to be reduced to ashes. The ashes were not even hot. It seemed that, somehow, he had the ability to expedite the entire burning process of many hours to a few milliseconds.

As everyone witnessed the mass destruction, Hanuman began to run in a totally different direction. When everyone was turning to him with hope, why was he abandoning them and fleeing? When the news of Hanuman having run away from the battlefield spread, the monkeys lost all hope. The only one who smiled in the midst of this chaos was Lakshmana. Because he was the only one who had seen Lord Rama whisper something into Hanuman's ears.

Suddenly, one monkey soldier shouted, 'Look! Look! Look where Hanuman has reached!'

All the other monkeys turned around and glanced at the direction this monkey was pointing to. They were fascinated and curious despite the impending danger. What was Hanuman up to?

Far away, they could see Hanuman climbing the fortress of Ravana. He had just jumped into the city. If he was running away, why was he running into the enemy camp? It was all a puzzle for the monkeys.

Suddenly, the monkeys saw their hero flying out of the fort holding on his back a huge plank of iron. As he was flying, he balanced the plank with one hand and tail. His other hand was navigating the flight. They couldn't figure out what Hanuman was trying to do. Lord Rama and Lakshmana exchanged a knowing glance.

Hanuman silently flew and landed right behind Bhasmalochana. By now, the monkeys were hiding behind rocks, trees, inside waterbodies—any possible place—to save themselves from the vicious glance of this demon. But more than their own safety, they were curious to know what Hanuman had in mind.

Hanuman's tail shot up carrying that iron plank high into the airway above Bhasmalochana's head. The tail expertly twisted and flipped the iron plank. Wow! What brilliance! Every monkey soldier that was attentive enough during that flip knew what was coming.

The tail began to lower the vertical iron plank in such a way that it came right in front of Bhasmalochana and blocked his vision. As soon as the plank landed on the ground, there was a classic blast.

KADABOOOM!

Bhasmalochana was now a heap of ashes.

The monkey army cheered and came running towards their saviour. Those who still didn't understand what exactly happened turned behind to see what that iron plank was.

It was a mirror!

Hanuman had made Bhasmalochana see himself!

The desire to burn others with your anger makes you forget to peep into the mirror. Before your anger burns others, it has burnt your tolerance.

Victory With Alphabets

This was a serious matter. Probably a toss-up between victory and defeat! If the God of Death himself comes and gives a warning, one had better take the warning seriously. From the time Yamaraj, the infallible God of Death, had visited Lord Rama and warned him about the latest strategy Ravana was cooking up in his camp and in the cauldron of his cruel brain, everyone was anxious.

Chandi stotra!

Whatever that meant! But the very name sent a jitter down the spine. What could be its consequence? It couldn't mean anything less than complete destruction of their entire army.

After a detailed discussion with Vibhishana, Lord Rama could clearly understand the gravity of the matter. He assigned this outlandish project to Hanuman with a totally unconventional instruction. 'Do what is needed; just stop this master plan of Ravana!'

Hanuman loved such instructions. The freedom that came with such instructions just pumped up his enthusiasm levels sky high. Now, he could use all his unconventional talents and ideas to serve Lord Rama. In a flash, he was sitting on the inner walls of Ravana's palace, assuming the form of a fly. His roving eyes were constantly making note of points and strategic locations that could help him make an exit at the appropriate time. Suddenly, a strange sound caught his attention. It was almost like a drone.

When he observed carefully, it came from a door that had slightly opened and was being stealthily closed. He had to make his decision soon. He made the leap and in a microsecond, before the door shut, made his entry into the room, squeezing his way through the fast shutting doorway. This was it! The venue of the Chandi stotra.

What Hanuman saw was shocking! Of all people in the universe, Brihaspati, the guru of the demigods was leading the recitation of the Chandi stotra. Why would he do that? Why would the guru of the demigods favour Ravana, and that too, secretly? One look around and it was quite obvious. There was stringent security around Brihaspati and it was clear that this wasn't a voluntary recitation.

Hanuman came zooming down and sat on the manuscript from which Brihaspati was reciting the slokas. Morphed into a fly, no one could detect his real identity. With his feet, he craftily rubbed off two words from the manuscript. Of course, this trick failed miserably when he realised that Brihaspati was hardly referring to the script. He had almost memorised the entire stotra except a few words here and there. The absence of the words was easily countered by Brihaspati's photographic memory.

Hanuman looked around carefully for some idea to impede this recitation. He noticed that though this section of the palace was sealed from outside, it was quite massive inside. In fact, it was designed like a very complicated maze. Exactly what he was looking for!

Hanuman quickly looked around at the guards who were stationed around Brihaspati. Seeing that their attention wasn't on Brihaspati and that they were casually stationed at their posts not expecting any sabotage, Hanuman decided to act. In an instant, Hanuman changed his form from that of a fly to a gigantic monster. Brihaspati was flabbergasted! He shrieked loudly and collapsed.

In that moment of panic, Hanuman withdrew his ghastly form and turned into a fly again. Panic prevailed now! Brihaspati was so scared that he began to run hither and thither. Wherever he ran, Hanuman would appear there in his ghastly form and scare him further. The guards couldn't figure out what was happening to the guru of the demigods. He had turned pale and was running like a mad man, screaming aloud and covering his eyes. Brihaspati ran into the maze and couldn't find his way back.

Amidst this commotion, Hanuman managed to delete three full verses from the script. The recitation turned chaotic and Brihaspati was in no position to continue. And even when Ravana forced him to complete the recitation, he omitted reciting those three verses. His memory failed him due to fear. When Ravana became aware of the mayhem, he personally came to redeem the recital. With his expertise in chanting, he tried to mollify the goddess, but in vain.

Ravana realised that the recital was a failure when nothing happened at the end of it. Instead of abandoning the entire effort, Ravana decided to do something even more drastic. Luckily, Hanuman had decided to hang around to understand Ravana's further plans. This time, Ravana performed a fire sacrifice to appease Goddess Chandi— something more effective than a mere recital. In a short while, a group of very trustworthy and scholarly brahmins were selected to perform this ritual.

As the brahmins were making their way to the ritual arena, a very enthusiastic young brahmin begged them to allow him to participate in this supremely auspicious and important yajna for the benefit of the kingdom and their King. His sincerity to help coupled with their need for assistance in such a massive sacrifice, was why they allowed him to accompany them. They did not repent their decision of inviting him. He was assisting each of them as if he had 10 hands. He was all over the place. As soon as any officiating brahmin asked him for an item, he handed it over immediately. His contribution was so significant that soon each of the brahmins was extremely pleased with this young boy. They blessed him and asked him to ask for anything that would please him.

'The opportunity to serve great souls is the greatest gift ever,' said the young brahmin.

This reply impressed them even more. Now they were more eager to bestow on him some tangible blessings or favours. They insisted that he ask for something immediately. Very reluctantly, he spoke up.

'If at all you are insistent that you want me to ask for something, let me ask you something that will benefit our King. I request you to make a small change in the final chant. Though the change seems small, it will benefit our master greatly. Substitute the letter "ha" by the letter "ka". That's all I want.' The young brahmin's genuine sincerity to serve their master and his attitude in serving them had pleased them so much that they didn't really think much about the implication of what he was saying. They did it!

Jaya tvam devi chamunde
Jaya bhutartha kaarini

Instead of saying *haarini* they said *kaarini*!
One small change and the result flipped.

The goddess was extremely annoyed with the sacrifice and her fiery eyes began to emit rays that destroyed the entire sacrifice. Everything in the vicinity was burnt to ashes.

The young brahmin walked out unscathed with a naughty smile on his lips. His form gradually changed to that of Hanuman and he flew out of Ravana's camp before anyone could find him.

The spirit of love doesn't exist in a grave but in a lively heart.
The spirit of language doesn't exist in words but in an enlivened heart.

Silencing the Kidnapper

A pigeon silently flew around the city of Lanka today. Not that pigeons didn't fly on other days. But this one seemed a very sneaky pigeon. It had come with a purpose to Lanka. It was quietly observing everything. Its target observation zone was the palace of Ravana. It managed to manoeuvre its way into the innermost section of the private discussion chamber of Ravana. What it saw shocked it beyond belief!

There was no time to waste now. There was nothing further to observe now. The pigeon flew 100 yojana across the ocean and landed at the feet of Lord Rama. Panting and huffing…

POOF!

The pigeon changed its form and in its place stood Vibhishana. His face clearly showed a sense of urgency. All the leaders had gathered realising the gravity of the situation.

'O Rama! There is grave danger to your life. Ravana has planned something that I was always apprehensive about. This, probably, will be our greatest test. Much more complicated than anything we can fathom. We have to combine all our wits and be really united.' All those present were trying to comprehend what his warnings really meant.

Lord Rama appeared very casual about the whole thing. He said in a very relaxed manner, 'I have full confidence in your wisdom, Jambavan's experience and Hanuman's abilities. I am happy to cooperate with anything you feel should be done.' And, Lord Rama walked away along with Lakshmana.

The entire monkey army got into action. It did initially seem to be a chaotic affair, but once everyone had settled down in their designated positions, it was clearly a brilliant strategy. The monkey army had been arranged in the form of a fort wall, with the centre kept vacant and clear. That way, every person in the army was stationed as one part of the wall and all eyes were fixed at the centre where Sugriva and Angad remained on guard. Once this was done, the execution of the second and more complex part of the plan began.

Hanuman and Vibhishana were the only people stationed outside the wall. Hanuman began to expand his tail. His tail began coiling around the army wall. After one complete circle, the tail extended even further and began to make another layer on top of the previous layer. In this way, layer after layer was created. Soon, the entire army was housed within the tail wall of Hanuman. A two-layered fort was created. Only a small opening was left to enable entry and exit into and out of the improvised fort. Hanuman personally guarded this entry.

When Lord Rama and Lakshmana returned from their stroll, they were mighty surprised with the intelligence of the army and also with their intense dedication to serve them at the cost of great personal inconvenience. Vibhishana guided them into the fort wall. As soon as Lord Rama and Lakshmana entered, the entire inner wall of monkeys bowed down in respect. Vibhishana explained that this system ensured protection from the sides, but the skies were still unguarded. He requested Lord Rama to invoke the Sudarshan Chakra to provide protection from the skies. With one gaze of Lord Rama, the Sudarshan Chakra of Lord Vishnu came gliding in. The effulgent disc began making its rounds, guarding the fort from the skyway.

With the most obvious directions being covered, Vibishana explained to Lord Rama that all this was just to make sure that Lord Rama and Lakshmana got good sleep that night. Lord Rama and Lakshmana laughed. This seemed to be the most complicated way to get good sleep. Their humour lightened the tense situation. Vibhishana had strategically placed Sugriva and Angad right at the centre of the fort wall, so that even if someone managed to sabotage every protective layer to reach Lord Rama, still, they would have two formidable superpowers to fight. Sugriva and Angad sat on the floor. Lord Rama and Lakshmana slept on the ground, resting their heads on the laps of the two monkey leaders.

Meanwhile, a dark shadow loomed around, well hidden from the views of thousands of watchful eyes. It was the most important part of Ravana's plan. In fact, it was Ravana's last plan. This was the King of Illusion, Mahiravana, in action. He was Ravana's friend from Patalaloka, the subterranean world. Vibhishana had by mistake stumbled upon the confidential meeting between Mahiravana with Ravana in Lanka. Every demon in the world knew of the illusory powers of Mahiravana. He had, in fact, captured Mayadevi, the illusory energy herself and imprisoned her.

As soon as he saw the fort made out of the tail of Hanuman and the Sudarshan Chakra blazing on top, he knew that Vibhishana was at work here. But for him,

Vibhishana had always been a child. And a child shows little foresight. Fort or no fort, Lord Rama and Lakshmana would disappear in no time. Thinking thus, Mahiravana began to move towards the fort.

As he walked, his form changed to that of King Dasaratha, the father of Lord Rama. He had noticed that Hanuman was stationed at the entry post, vigilantly guarding the access, while Vibhishana patrolled around. The morphed King Dasaratha made his entry as soon as Vibhishana had passed by Hanuman and turned around the corner.

'O monkey, I am King Dasaratha. I am here to meet my sons, Rama and Lakshmana. It's been so many years now. I was unable to wait for their return to Ayodhya. I heard they are inside this tail fort. Would you be kind enough to permit me entry to be with my sons?' These words of King Dasaratha struck a chord with Hanuman. Vibhishana's words began echoing... *He is a master of illusion...*

Not wanting to take any risk, and at the same time not willing to be disrespectful to King Dasaratha, Hanuman chose a safe approach. 'Let Vibhishana come. He is in charge of this fort. Once he permits, I will escort you in.'

Hearing these words, King Dasaratha excused himself, saying that he would come back in a few minutes till Vibhishana returns. When Vibhishana came around, Hanuman narrated the visit of King Dasaratha. Vibhishana immediately became alert and said, 'Even if your father comes, don't let him in unless I sanction it.' With this stern warning, he walked away, patrolling all directions.

As soon as Vibhishana left, Bharata, the brother of Lord Rama came. He made the same plea to visit Lord Rama. Hanuman humbly repeated the request to wait till Vibhishana returns. Bharata left in a hurry. When

Vibhishana returned and was informed of the arrival of Bharata, he repeated the same instruction. 'Even if your father comes, don't let him in unless I sanction it.'

After a while, Kaushalya, the mother of Lord Rama came and went. Then Maharaj Janaka, the father of Sita came. When Hanuman wouldn't permit him to enter the fort, he began an argument with Hanuman. Just then, a loud roar was heard and suddenly, Janaka sheepishly scurried away. Vibhishana emerged from the other end of the fort, smiling at his accomplishment. Again, he warned Hanuman, 'Even if your father comes, don't let him in unless I sanction it.'

Vibhishana left again for another patrolling session. After this experience, Hanuman decided that now whoever would come, he would lock them till Vibhishana returned. If this was indeed Mahiravana in disguise, it would be better to capture him at the earliest. Just them Vibhishana returned again. Hanuman was puzzled. How did he manage to return so quickly? He had hardly turned the corner.

Seeing the puzzled expression on Hanuman's face, Vibhishana said, 'O Hanuman, I have realised that this night is going to be more complicated than I had estimated. Lord Rama and Lakshmana will need more protection than what our watchful eyes can provide. I have a special holy thread that I want to tie around their arms to protect them from any evil. You had better be alert while I tie this on the brothers and return. Mahiravana is in full action now.'

Saying this and giving a pat on Hanuman's back, Vibhishana entered the fort with a sly smile leaving Hanuman confused. Hanuman still couldn't decode anything. Everything seemed illusory today!

Stepping into the fort, Vibhishana walked to the centre where the princes were resting. He opened his palms and placed them horizontally in front of his face and blew out air from his mouth while spinning in all directions. The fine pink dust shot out at great speed. Before they could even react, every monkey standing there fell unconscious. Sugriva and Angad didn't even have the time to rise up from their sitting positions before the dust hit their nostrils.

The clamour of the monkey army falling with their weapons was clearly audible outside the fort. Hanuman panicked. He wanted to rush in, but he couldn't abandon his post. Just then, Vibhishana returned from his patrolling! What was happening here? He had just entered. If this was Vibhishana, then who had entered? If the one who had entered was Vibhishana, then who was this? Who was who?

Hanuman caught Vibhishana by his shoulders and began to shake him violently. 'If you are here, then who went in to tie the holy thread on Lord Rama's arms? Who are you? Was all this your plan to capture Lord Rama and make Ravana victorious? You have acted as a well-wisher. You are after all a demon. Why have you done this?'

Instantly, Vibhishana became concerned about the welfare of Lord Rama. But Hanuman held him down tightly. He couldn't even move an inch. He tried to muster all his convincing powers, 'Hanuman, try to understand, I am the real Vibhishana. The one who went in was Mahiravana. Lord Rama is in trouble. If I have deceived Lord Rama in any way, let me be held guilty of the sin of killing a brahmin or a cow.'

Hanuman wasn't impressed with Vibhishana's declaration. Why would a demon be bothered about the death of a brahmin or a cow? Realising that Hanuman wasn't buying his innocence, he spoke further trying to clarify. 'Hanuman, think clearly. How can I be a spy of

Ravana? How many officers of Ravana have I helped you kill? How many plans of Ravana have I helped you thwart. I even allowed my own son to die in the battle. What more do you need as proof of my sincerity? This is not the time to doubt, but serve Lord Rama in cooperation. Lord Rama needs us now!'

Finding merit in Vibhishana's words, Hanuman loosened his grip and remorse filled his heart. He had committed a major blunder. Not only had he allowed the wrong person to enter, but he had doubted the right person.

Grasping the seriousness of the situation, Vibhishana entered the fort and Hanuman followed shortly after recoiling his tail, and thus, dismantling the fort. The scene that greeted them was agonising. Every monkey was lying unconscious. Right at the centre, Sugriva and Angad lay asleep, legs, crossed indicating they hadn't even got a chance to stand up. What was most painful was that Lord Rama and Lakshmana were missing. In the place where they had been resting, there was an endless tunnel. Vibhishana broke down and began wailing loudly, claiming that all hope was lost.

Though sad and dejected, Hanuman helped all the monkey soldiers become conscious by sprinkling water on their faces. Soon, all the monkeys were crying at the loss of their very life. None of them could think clearly. Jambavan spoke up, 'Let us send Hanuman in search of Lord Rama. There is no realm that is inaccessible to him.'

Every monkey agreed that only Hanuman is the friend of the distressed. After receiving the blessings of everyone present, Hanuman dived headlong into the tunnel. For the initial few yojana, it was a free fall, but beyond that a force began to suck him in. The speed of travel escalated beyond comprehension. It was too fast even for the son of Vayu.

Suddenly, he was thrown off the grid and he landed on the ground. The force was such that he rolled for a while before he could regain balance. As soon as Hanuman realised what was about to happen to him, he took the shape of a regular monkey to withstand the fall and balance faster.

Looking around, he found himself in the magical city of Patalaloka. Stealthily, he climbed a tree to survey the foreign land. As soon as he climbed, a branch snapped and fell with a thud, attracting attention. Suddenly, all eyes were on the little monkey.

One man said, 'This is the first time I am seeing a monkey in Patalaloka. I wonder where he came from?'

An old lady, who had been observing from a distance, walked up to the tree and dramatically expressed. 'Our King is dead. This city is finished!' Hearing this, a crowd gathered around her. She was pointing out to the monkey and beating her chest. Since a group gathered around her to hear what she had to say, she continued with her melodrama. 'Our King has a secret that he has been hiding from us. He is under a curse. The curse said that the day human beings and monkeys enter this city, the King will be dead and the city shall be doomed. Just this morning, I heard that the King had received two handsome men and now this monkey has entered the city. I say wind up your business and leave the city immediately. Save yourself and let the King save himself.'

The monkey beamed with joy. The two handsome men had to be Lord Rama and Lakshmana. As confusion prevailed amongst the onlookers, he slipped out of view. He leapt from tree to tree and reached a beautiful lake. There, he found many women who had come to fetch water. A group was animatedly gossiping. He began to eavesdrop on their conversation.

'What's going on in the palace today? Why do we hear music emanating from the inner sections of the palace? I have never seen so many brahmins go in and gleefully as if they were being amply rewarded. Could you please share the inside news?' one inquisitive girl was asking an elderly lady who was working in the inner chambers of the palace.

'Shhhh.... This is highly confidential. Don't dare tell anyone. There is going to be a special sacrifice in the evening to Goddess Mahamaya. A human sacrifice! The King has kidnapped two extremely handsome human beings. I have never seen anyone with that kind of beauty in this life. Sad, they will be dead soon. Anyway, I must go now. Lots of special duties have been assigned today. But please make sure that you keep this information confidential till evening. Please, I earnestly request you. It's a matter of my life.' Saying this, the elderly lady scampered away into the palace, hurriedly looking here and there, ensuring no one had eavesdropped on this conversation.

Hanuman realised he had to act fast. He was racing against time. He had no clue about the magical city. How would he ever know where Lord Rama and Lakshmana had been held hostage? He was running in every direction, trying to get some hint, unable to figure out anything. The palace was indeed mysterious. Even the doors and windows were mysterious. Hanuman tried coming in front of the walls when no one was looking, but to no avail. It seemed that the walls would become doors only for a select few. As Hanuman was completely confused about his next step, a wall opened up. An idea walked out of the door!

Bound in iron chains, a middle-aged lady walked out of the palace, ushered by a team of armed guards on all sides. By her attire, it appeared she was part of the royalty. But from the chains that bound her hands, it was obvious that she was a prisoner. The soldiers were looking all around to ensure that everything was safe. From the nervous look on the lady's face, it was clear that she didn't like doing what she was being pushed to do. The entourage was walking towards the lakeside. That's when Hanuman noticed something peculiar in one of the soldier's hand. An earthen pot!

As they reached the lake, that soldier handed over the earthen pot to the lady. She held it uncomfortably in her palms and said something to the soldiers. They looked at one another and exchanged opinions. After a brief animated conversation, they arrived at a conclusion. One of them came forward and unlocked her handcuffs. With her hands free, she turned towards the lake and squatted. She gently placed the pot on the banks of the lake and sat down with hands folded.

Hanuman took on a miniscule form and sat on the rim of the pot in front of her and observed her carefully. She had closed her eyes and was offering a prayer. Once she was done, she opened her eyes and muttered something under her breath. Of course, Hanuman's sharp ears caught it. She said, 'What a sad situation I am in? My brother is a completely useless demon. I can't believe that he is going to sacrifice such handsome princes today. O Goddess, please protect Lord Rama and Lakshmana. They don't deserve to die such a miserable death.'

Instantly, Hanuman spoke, 'Do you know where Lord Rama and Lakshmana are? Will you please help me find them?'

Initially, she couldn't find the source of the voice. She looked around anxiously. She was shocked to see the tiny monkey on the rim of her earthen pot. She looked at him with suspicion and said, 'Are you Ravana in disguise; this is how you keep a watch on me?'

Hanuman spoke up mustering all his sincerity and innocence, 'O Mother, please don't doubt me. I am not any demon but a humble servant of Lord Rama. I am here to rescue him.'

Hanuman's reply gave her great joy—something that had gone out of her life. 'Oh, I am so happy to hear this. If you can manage to rescue Lord Rama, I am almost sure that the life of my son and my own will also be saved. Though I am Duratandi, the sister of Mahiravana, I am a prisoner in my own home.'

'Mother, if you help me, I will help you.' Hanuman was happy to serve and realised that this lady was in genuine need of help. He was curious to know what calamity could have landed Mahiravana's sister in this perplexing situation. She revealed a stunning story. 'Many years ago when my son, Nilamega, was born, an unembodied voice from the higher realms had declared that this boy would be the future King of Patalaloka when Mahiravana dies. This news antagonised my brother so much that he imprisoned us that very day. My son has grown up and spent all his life in jail and hasn't even experienced the outside world yet.'

Though this tale was definitely interesting, Hanuman wanted to know how the magical demon allowed her to venture out to fetch water today. She explained that she had a unique boon that if any ritual is performed using the water that she personally fetches, then, it would surely be a grand success. This water that she was carrying was to be used during the sacrificial ceremony of Lord Rama and Lakshmana.

As soon as Hanuman heard this, he grinned naughtily. He told her that he would hide behind a mango leaf that she should set afloat on the water inside the pot. Though she seemed to accept the idea, she was worried about how to tackle the hate-detecting yantra (device) in the palace. Every person who entered the palace had to pass through this device. It had a scale that could detect the hate levels of the person under inspection. The device could accurately determine the degree of hate the person nursed against Mahiravana. Hanuman assured her that there was no need to worry and that he would take care of everything. All she had to do was be extremely confident in whatever she did.

Now, the drama began. She picked up the pot, filled it with water and put the mango leaf, on to which Hanuman had clung, into the pot. With the pot hoisted on her head, she began to walk slowly towards the unsuspecting soldiers. The first wall opened and they entered the palace. Hanuman peeped out and saw they were approaching the machine. He tried his best to develop positive thoughts about Mahiravana so that he goes undetected. As she crossed the machine, all kinds of sirens began to blaze across directions. The guards began to panic. Duratandi began to tremble.

'Who hates Mahiravana so much here? Why are you trembling so much? We know that you don't like your brother, but your hatred level has never been so high. What happened today?' As one soldier was questioning her, the machine went into a frenzy and eventually broke down.

'How can that happen? How can such a perfect machine break down like this? Surely, there must be someone hiding in the pot. Bring it down. Let us inspect it. With trembling hands, Duratandi lowered the pot and the curious soldiers glanced inside. Carefully shifting the mango leaf aside, they inspected the contents of the pot. 'Nothing! It's just water.'

Concluding that the machine must have become defective, they permitted her to enter with the pot.

She was escorted straight up to the place where the sacrifice was to be made in a few hours. As soon as she placed the pot on the ground, a wasp flew out of it and began to hover around her. The wasp flew all the way till the deity Mahamaya and hovered around for some time. Then it returned to Duratandi. She silently got up and walked away. The wasp followed her closely. Soon, she was locked into her prison cell again. Now, in the privacy of the cell walls, Hanuman questioned her about Mahiravana in detail and learnt every secret she knew about him. Equipped with valuable information from Duratandi, the wasp flew away.

Hovering around the prison structure of Mahiravana, Hanuman finally spotted the cell where Lord Rama and Lakshmana had been held captive. Tears welling up in his eyes, he flew straight into the cell and fell at the feet of Lord Rama. When Lord Rama realised that it was his dear associate Hanuman, he became very joyful. They quickly exchanged notes and Hanuman left. It was time for action now!

Before fully believing the far-fetched information that Duratandi shared with him, he decided to verify all the facts. And the only way to do so was through direct conflict with Mahiravana. The search for Mahiravana's private abode wasn't very difficult, mostly because it was the most opulent one. When Hanuman reached near the palace, a surprise greeted him.

There was only one guard standing in front of the palace and watchfully patrolling the palace. He was half-monkey and half-crocodile! Since Hanuman had assumed a very tiny form, there was hardly any scope of anyone spotting him.

Confident about his disguise, he tried entering the doors of Mahiravana's chambers through the slight gap below the door. The guard put his foot right in front of Hanuman, sealing the gap neatly. He had been caught!

Seeing no point in retaining his minuscule form, Hanuman assumed his original look. The guard readied himself for a combat. Looking at the war-pose of the guard, Hanuman felt he looked familiar. So Hanuman enquired from the guard who he was. The reply stunned him beyond imagination. He said, 'I am Makharadwaja, the son of Hanuman.'

'What? How can you be my son? I never looked at a woman with lust, let alone marry and beget a child.' Hanuman was flabbergasted with this revelation.

'I was told that when Hanuman burnt the city of Lanka, a drop of his sweat fell into the ocean and a crocodile consumed that. I was born from the belly of that very crocodile. So, I guess you are my father. But, whatever our relation is, I am now the guard of Mahiravana and I cannot allow anyone to enter his abode without his sanction. So, please do not embarrass me into defeating my own father in combat.' Makharadwaja was quite frank.

Hanuman didn't wait for another moment. In the next few seconds, Makharadwaja only saw a series of fists and legs and he suffered an extreme degree of pain in various parts of his body. Soon, he was lying on the ground on his stomach, all tied up. His arms and legs were securely fastened and his mouth gagged. Leaving his son in this state, Hanuman resumed his minuscule form and flew through the doors of Mahiravana's private abode in style.

Mahiravana was seated and in deep contemplation. Suddenly, Hanuman resumed his regular form, drew out a sword and struck Mahiravana on his head and sliced him into two halves. Mahiravana was dead! Blood and gore lay all over the floor. It was a mess!

It's over! Hanuman couldn't believe that he had finished this powerful demon with just one stroke. He was very happy that this ordeal was finally over. He stepped back to return to Lord Rama when he heard a weird sound. He turned just in time to see Mahiravana rushing towards him with a raised sword. Hanuman somersaulted in the nick of time and successfully evaded the brutal strike. Mahiravana lost his balance, tripped and fell headlong. The sword slipped from his hand. Hanuman grabbed the sword instantly, and began to chop Mahiravana mercilessly. He hit with such power that pieces from Mahiravana's body were thrown here and there. Soon, all that remained were pieces of the demon's flesh scattered all over.

Satisfied that this was the final episode in the book of this demon's life, Hanuman began to find his way back. No sooner had Hanuman taken a few steps away from the bloody mess, than he heard a sound again. He was back! How did this man return from the dead every single time? How was it possible that despite being cut into countless pieces, he was alive again?

What he had heard about him was true after all! No matter how many times he is killed, he will return to life again. No point in continuing to fight him in the regular style, thought Hanuman. Hanuman assumed his minuscule form again and escaped from the palace.

As soon as Mahiravana understood that Hanuman had arrived to rescue Lord Rama and Lakshmana, he decided to re-schedule the sacrificial ritual. He ran out towards the sacrificial arena at the temple of Mahamaya and began to bark out instructions to his soldiers and servants. Everyone began to run hither and thither to get things moving. Lord Rama and Lakshmana were brought and tied around poles. As soon as Lord Rama and Lakshmana saw that they were being ushered in much before the stipulated time, they realised Hanuman had succeeded in the first phase of the plan and began hoping that Hanuman could make it back on time. Everything depended on his speed.

While the preparations were in full swing, Hanuman had reached a cave hundreds of yojana away from the sacrificial arena. This was the cave Duratandi had told him about and which he had reconfirmed from Mahamaya. He had an important mission in this cave the consequence of which would determine the next course of events in Mahiravana' palace.

This cave was unique; it had five entrances. There was no time to think. It didn't matter how many entrances there were, all he had to do was blow out five flames. He ran into one of the entrances and at the far end was a blazing flame. With one hard blow, the flame was extinguished. He then quickly ran back and entered the second entrance and blew out that flame. Sequentially, he blew out all the five flames. Once done, he was happy with his performance. However, when he returned to the first entrance, Hanuman was shocked to see the rear wall all lit up. Every entrance he peeped in, he was greeted with the same sight.

He kept running in and out of the five caves entries, blowing out the flames but they kept coming back. After multiple attempts, Hanuman was fed up.

He closed his eyes and invoked his father Vayu and sought his advice. The Wind God revealed that all the five flames had to be extinguished at once. Hanuman turned back to his mission. He stood right in the middle of the five caves and closed his eyes. Instantly, four more heads grew on the shoulders of Hanuman. The first was that of a ferocious lion, the second was that of Garuda the eagle, the third resembled a black-complexioned boar, and the forth was that of a horse. The fifth was his original monkey-faced head. With these five heads, Hanuman roared fiercely. The roar was thunderous and shook up the mountains with its vibrations. He blew so hard that not only were all the five flames extinguished at once, but, literally, the entire back wall of the cave was blown away.

Hanuman took off again. He had an emergency flight now!

Meanwhile, Mahiravana had untied Lord Rama and Lakshmana. He got them down right in front of the deity Mahamaya. After many incantations and chanting scores of mantras, he asked Lord Rama to bend down and get ready to die in the sacrifice. Lord Rama feigned innocence. He told Mahiravana that since he was a prince and had been raised in a royal palace, he had no idea how to bend. He requested Mahiravana to show him exactly how to bend and then it would be easy for him to follow suit. Mahiravana was disgusted at Lord Rama's ignorance. Nonetheless, he agreed to demonstrate personally, since this was an important sacrifice for him.

He fell on his knees and placed his head on the wooden altar at the exact slot for the neck. Doing that, he closed his eyes to show Lord Rama how he should position himself. As soon as Mahiravana closed his eyes, Lord Rama picked up the sacrificial sword that was placed close by and beheaded Mahiravana. At that very instant, Lakshmana ran across the temple room, climbed up a wall, broke open a door and smashed a diamond that was kept within the closed doors. Exactly at that time, Hanuman flew into the temple room.

With all the three tasks accomplished simultaneously, Mahiravana's head did not rejoin his body this time. He was finally dead!

The three heroes came together and embraced each other. It was indeed a happy moment. Suddenly, the whole building they were housed in began to vibrate. The floor below them was quaking. Something was wrong here...

Hanuman expanded himself. Lord Rama and Lakshmana sat on his muscular shoulders. He began to run at the speed of the wind, dodging falling pillars and walls. Somehow, he managed to exit the palace which caved in soon after. Hanuman kept running at the pace of wind. The catastrophe wasn't over yet. The entire city was collapsing now. He began to run towards the very spot he had entered Patalaloka. As soon as he found that, he jumped in carrying the two brothers. And suddenly, they began to be sucked upwards.

They were thrown upwards and the suction force withdrew abruptly. They fell on the ground. As soon as they were off the suction grid, the tunnel shut down permanently. They opened their eyes to see thousands of happy faces. They were back amongst their friends and well-wishers.

The monkey army had a lot to ask and the three of them had a lot to tell. The entire night passed in storytelling—a story they had never heard before!

An insecure heart measures hate levels in others. A secure heart takes measures to increase love in oneself.

A Crocodile Speaks

'You fool! Are you part of the enemy camp? How dare you advise me?' Ravana was boiling in anger. He was so flustered with Kalanemi's proposal that he threw his helmet to the ground, shattering it.

Kalanemi had only tried to help his master. He knew that Ravana's life was at stake because he lacked good advisors. And he shunned those who gave him good advice.

Ravana had called for Kalanemi the moment he heard of Hanuman's departure to Dronachal to procure medicinal herbs for Lakshmana who had been incapacitated by Meghnad's weapon. Whether Hanuman got the herbs wasn't as important as whether he got it at the right time. Delay in getting the herb meant denial of life for Lakshmana. Ravana's proposal to Kalanemi was that the latter should approach Hanuman in the guise of a sage and delay his return. According to Ravana, the sage trick always worked with people who were too emotional by nature.

Instead of immediately following the instruction and praising his wit, Kalanemi launched a long-winding sermon on righteousness and what Ravana should be doing. After that, it was only natural for Ravana to react the way he did.

What else could you expect from a King who had never paid heed to what others had to say?

Having no choice, Kalanemi proceeded to the north recalling the sacrifice made by Maricha. Surely, he was going to follow in the footsteps of Maricha soon. On the route to Dronachal, he fashioned a beautiful hermitage on a mountain next to a river. He was sure that Hanuman would take the aerial route above this very mountain. He lit a sacrificial fire and was confident that its scented smoke would attract Hanuman's attention. To make it even more plausible, he had multiple demons disguised as sages, sitting around the fire and chanting.

The smoke did catch Hanuman's attention as he was speeding across the sky. Two things compelled Hanuman to descend to the hermitage for a short visit. One was to find out how he had missed such a beautiful and vibrant hermitage during his previous visit. He, in fact, was in doubt whether he was on the right track or had lost his sense of direction. He, thus, felt compelled to descend and clarify the direction to his destination. And the second reason was that he was quite thirsty at this point in time. He was desperately looking for water.

Descending at the door of the hermitage, he saw the demon-sage absorbed in intense worship. The sage came out of his ritual to acknowledge the guest and enquired how he could serve him and what made him visit this out-of-the-world hermitage. Hanuman revealed the purpose of his visit and requested for some water. As the demon-sage handed over a glass of water to Hanuman, he began to speak very sweetly to him. He said, 'My brave Hanuman, you don't have to worry anymore. I have good news for you. I am *tri-kal-jnani*, I can clearly see the past, present and future.

Lakshmana is revived! There is a celebration in your camp. Lord Rama managed to revive Lakshmana by his mere glance. You can now stay here for some more time and enjoy our hospitality. These forests are known for their juicy fruits and nectarine water sources.'

Something didn't seem right here. Hanuman decided to play along till things become clearer. Despite drinking the glass of water, his thirst wasn't quenched. He needed a lot more. In fact, this was Hanuman's typical style of functioning. When he was engaged in service, he would totally forget his bodily needs. But when he realised that his body needed some nourishment, he would consume a huge amount at one go. Now he needed to quench his thirst once and for all, till the war was over. With that in mind, he asked to be shown a reservoir of water.

The sage assigned a young sage to assist Hanuman in finding the way to a nearby lake. As they were leaving, the demon-sage Kalanemi whispered into Hanuman's ears a secret. 'I am giving you a tip that will quench your thirst forever. When you drink water from the lake, make sure that you keep your eyes tightly shut. I will take care of the rest. Also, once you return, I will share with you a special mantra that will help you identify all the special herbs on Mount Dronachal.'

As instructed, Hanuman entered the lake and drank the water with his eyes tightly closed. Suddenly, he sensed a movement to his left. The next instant, a huge crocodile attacked him. While continuing to drink water with his right hand, Hanuman fought with the crocodile with his left hand. With a few quick powerful thrusts and twists, he managed to tear apart the mouth of the crocodile, killing it instantly. From the dead crocodile appeared a brilliant spark that transformed into a celestial nymph who paid her respects to Hanuman.

'Respected Hanuman, I was an apsara in the heavenly realms. Since I offended a sage, I was cursed to accept the body of a crocodile. Take my warning seriously, Hanuman, this sage is a fraud. He has sinister plans for you. Act wisely!' And she disappeared.

Quickly returning to the hermitage, Hanuman thanked the sage for his hospitality and reported that according to his instructions, he drank the water with closed eyes. The sage was perplexed on his return. But there was plan B if the crocodile attack failed. He called Hanuman closer so that he could whisper the sacred confidential mantra into his ears. With folded hands, Hanuman went close and said, 'My dear Master, before I accept the holy mantra from you, I would like to offer you my guru dakshina. Only when I please my guru will the mantra bear fruit.'

Kalanemi was visibly pleased and was eager to receive his guru dakshina. Hanuman clenched his fist and gave a powerful punch on his jaws. That very instant, Kalanemi came out of his disguise and assumed his original demonic form. Hanuman ran up to him and delivered another flying punch. The second punch was so hard that Kalanemi vomited blood and died.

With an illusory obstacle cleared, Hanuman proceeded to Dronachal and obtained the life-saving herbs from the holy mountains. The venture to obtain herbs saved Lakshmana and finished off Kalanemi.

Spirituality is a balance between resisting temptations and savouring nourishment. On the one hand, Hanuman was fighting with the crocodile that represented temptations. And on the other hand, he was drinking water that represented nourishment. A happy spiritualist knows that both are not to be done exclusively, but, simultaneously.

Outwitting the Sun God

There was a crisis on this side but a celebration on that side. There was wailing on this side and victory cries on that side. Ravana was happy and Lord Rama was sad.

Lakshmana had been brutally attacked by Ravana's fatal weapon—known as Shela—fashioned by Mayadanava. Though a cure was available, it would take a good few hours even if Hanuman were to travel at the speed of lightning. Jambavan had warned Hanuman to return by sunrise at any cost. With sunrise, Lakshmana's life would wane. The weapon had been programmed to create havoc in accordance with the movements of the sun and sunrise would mark the beginning of its strongest effect that would be impossible to endure.

Understanding the paucity of time, Hanuman made a mental note of the herbs that he was supposed to bring and leapt without further delay. As soon as he was airborne, Hanuman realised the catastrophe that awaited him. Impossible! How could this happen? The sun was rising at midnight!

From the altitude that he was in, Hanuman gazed towards the Lankan palaces and could see Ravana laughing his guts out. Instantly, Hanuman could comprehend what had transpired behind this supernatural phenomenon. Ravana had dared to meddle with the systems of nature.

Hanuman took a detour and instead of proceeding towards the mountains to find the life-saving herb, he soared towards the sun. As he was zooming ahead, a flashback of his childhood days hit his mind. He had taken this same route many years ago. Back then, he was eagerly rushing towards the sun to enjoy a fruit and so many years later history was repeating itself. But now, he was rushing to save a life. Back then, he thought about satisfying his own needs and now, he lived for satisfying others' needs.

As soon as Hanuman reached, with one kick he disgorged Aruna, the charioteer of the Sun God. Aruna was blown a few yojana away. The Sun God was flabbergasted. What's going on here? One look at Hanuman and he realised that this was the same person who had attacked him as a child. His anger transformed into fear now. With folded hands, he spoke to Hanuman.

'What do you want from me? Please don't trouble me again. I am only doing my duties.' Hearing the Sun God plead this way, Hanuman spoke up.

'You are lying! How is it your duty to rise at midnight? How can you alter the laws of nature?'

The Sun God was now in a fix. He was stuck between the devil and the deep blue sea.

Perplexed, the Sun God peeped below and saw Ravana signalling him with a wave of his hands to rise fast. He begged Hanuman, 'Please understand my predicament. I want to help Lord Rama in his mission. But I am so fearful of Ravana. No one can survive the wrath of that demon. All the gods shiver at his very sight.'

Hanuman became thoughtful for a while. Suddenly, he smiled, 'I got it! I have a great idea that can help both. Your name is Bhanu and my name is Hanu, so, both of us are alike. If you follow what I say, you can satisfy both sides aptly. Ravana wouldn't be angry with you and Lord Rama will be pleased with you.'

The Sun God became curious, 'Tell me, O clever Hanuman! What should I do now?'

With a naughty grin Hanuman said, 'Come closer, lend me your ears and I will whisper my idea to you.'

The Sun God unwittingly came closer to Hanuman and bent low, bringing his ears close for Hanuman to whisper. Hanuman put his arms around the Sun God as if holding him to whisper into his ears. As soon as his arms were firmly fixed around the Sun God's neck, he tightened his grip and locked the Sun God in his armpit.

The Sun God struggled to get out of his grip, but in vain. He was totally helpless within the vice-like grip of Hanuman. With the sun under his armpit, Hanuman began to fly towards the mountains. Everyone including Ravana who witnessed this was left dumbfounded.

As Hanuman was flying, his armpit glowed with the sun's effulgence. He managed to get the herbs and revive Lakshmana; now that time was his captive, it was needless to say that he made it on time.

The Sun God, even with his pain and embarrassment, was happy. Fearing embarrassment from Ravana, he chose to go with the wrong side, but then he was forced to be on the side of the righteous by virtue of another embarrassment.

Fear is the black hole into which clear thinking disappears.

The Treasure Hunt

'What's happening? How in the world could this be possible?' The monkey army was flabbergasted by what they had witnessed.

For the last hour or so, Lord Rama was severing every limb of Ravana's body one by one. Every head on Ravana's shoulders had been hacked off. Every hand had been lopped off. But the astounding thing was that every time he did that, the limb would reconnect instantly. He even tried throwing the detached limb at a great distance and in opposite directions and even into the ocean. The detached limb would fly back and rejoin, as if, magnetically attracted by some unknown force.

'It's impossible to kill him like this. Try as you may, nothing conventional will work on him,' Ravana's brother Vibhishana advised Lord Rama, who was failing repeatedly in his attempts to destroy Ravana.

Putting his assault to a brief halt, Lord Rama turned towards Vibhishana and enquired with concern. 'What else can I do? Do you have a better idea?'

'If I may, I would like to share a secret about Ravana's powers that only we three siblings know of.' The eagerness of Lord Rama and the monkey leaders that had gathered around him right in the middle of the war, prodded Vibhishana to continue. 'Lord Brahma had offered Ravana a boon-bane when we performed severe austerities. What you see is Lord Brahma's boon in action! Even if he is cut into pieces and the pieces are scattered in a million different directions, his body will reassemble instantaneously. No one can undo this boon. But we can focus on the bane which was also a part of the contract.'

Now, everyone were all ears, ready to comprehend the magnitude of the impossible task that lay ahead.

'At that time, Lord Brahma fashioned an arrow called the Brahmabana. He directed that unless that arrow is shot into the belly of Ravana, his death is impossible. No other weapon will be fruitful in causing his destruction. And even this weapon, if aimed at any place other than his belly, would prove futile. With this kind of coded protection, Ravana knew that he was practically immortal. His only task was to make sure that he hides the arrow in a place where even the wind can't enter. And that he has done astutely.' When Vibhishana concluded, there was only one question on everyone's mind. 'Who will do it?'

Realising Lord Rama's predicament, Hanuman quipped, 'My Lord, please allow me to serve you in this venture. I will locate the arrow and deposit it in your custody soon.'

'Here is a clue. Ravana's wife Mandodari is the only person who knows where that arrow is. Needless to say, the quarters of Mandodari fall under the highest security zone of Lanka.' Vibhishana smiled and Hanuman got his hint from that sly smile.

'Jai Shri Rama!' With a loud cry, Hanuman took off on his adventure landing straight into a desolate section of

Lanka. In a second, he transformed into an old astrologer. His mace became his astrological treatise that he carried under his arms. He wobbled around the city undetected. He held a walking stick in his right hand and wore a clean but simple-looking white garment. The red tilak on his forehead shone brilliantly in the sunlight. His cheeks drooped, revealing his fragile age. The wrinkles around his eyes were signs of his wisdom and experience.

'Jai Shrimaan Ravana!' With every step, he recited this sacred mantra. Seeing his stature, the already tense people of Lanka began to come to him to get their charts read. He would sit on street corners and read several horoscopes. Every finding of his was on the dot. His words became a salve for their anxious burning hearts.

Slowly, he began edging closer to the main palace. Soon, the queen heard about this wonder astrologer who was an ardent devotee of her husband. She was eager to have an audience with him. Rejecting the gorgeously ornate lion throne that was always offered to elevated guests, the astrologer chose to sit on the floor on a kusa grass mat. This one action convinced Mandodari that this was the perfect person to give her an honest and clear prediction about Lanka's future. This war was already getting painful. She had almost lost everyone who was dear to her. Yet, there was hope till her husband was alive. But what would be the future of Lankeshwara?

'The future is either black or white. Either Ravana will rule forever or he will die today.' Intensely absorbed in his astrological books, he spoke with concern in his eyes.

'How can we make sure that victory is ours? Tell me. Tell me. Is there anything we can do? Tell me…tell me…'

Mandodari panicked hearing the clarity with which he spoke those words.

'The secret that you hold in this house will save you as long as it's a secret.' The mysterious astrologer spoke looking at her, his eyes lifting his gaze from the astrological books.

'Secret! What secret are you talking about?' She acted totally surprised. She was actually confused. How could anyone know such deep secrets? That too, a total stranger whom she had just met! She hoped against hope that he was talking about something else.

'Don't fool me! I know everything: past, present and future. I just want to warn you because I am concerned about the welfare of our able King. Don't rely on anyone. Even if Lord Brahma comes himself, don't reveal the treasure to him.' Saying this, the old man got up and began to stagger towards the gate. He walked a few steps and turned slowly to face her again.

There were worry lines visible on her face, 'Are you sure it's safe enough? Vibhishana is aware of every nook and cranny of this palace. What if he actually knows the whereabouts of this treasure which has become your life now?'

Mandodari seemed confident yet concerned at the same time. She said, 'No no. He can never know unless I tell him. But since this is a question of my husband's life, no precaution is enough. I totally trust you to help me find the best place to house it secretly. Right now it's inside this glass pillar. Where should I...'

CRAAAAAACK!

'Jai Shri Rama!' Even before Mandodari could complete her sentence, Hanuman kicked at the glass pillar shattering it and quickly grabbed the arrow and dashed out of the palace.

Everything happened so quickly that none of the soldiers had a chance to react, let alone stop Hanuman.

WHOOOOSH!

With one arrow, Ravana was history!

Decoding another's password is easier than decoding another's intention.

A Delayed Flight

Covering the distance of thousands of yojana in a few minutes, Hanuman was hovering over Mount Kailash. If there was any place in the world he would find a Shiva Linga, it was here. But despite laboriously searching for it in every corner of the mountain range, Hanuman was disappointed. He was very well aware of Lord Rama's hurry to return to Ayodhya on time. Bharata had warned of dire consequences, if Lord Rama delayed his return even by a few hours after the 14 years of exile. The countdown had begun and time was ticking away. Bharata's life was in danger. But Lord Rama wasn't going to return unless he had performed a thanksgiving ritual, offering his gratitude to Lord Shiva, the Lord of Destruction.

Hanuman could find no alternative than to sit down and invoke the presence of his divine father Lord Shiva by his intense meditative calling. A couple of hours went by and lo and behold, Lord Shiva made his appearance and offered Hanuman a Shiva Linga with his own hands. Hanuman lost no time in flying back to the southern shore of the land with the newly-acquired Linga.

Upon reaching, what he saw brought tears to his eyes. How could Lord Rama do that? Someone else had already brought a Shiva Linga and Lord Rama, without considering the trouble Hanuman had taken, had even finished performing the ritual on that Linga. All his efforts had gone to waste. What was the point in acquiring the original Linga from Lord Shiva himself when Lord Rama was ready to accept a regular one? He felt humiliated and sad. Lord Rama explained to him that the time for his return was drawing near and the auspicious ritual had to be performed within the stipulated time and, therefore, he was forced to take this tough call. Hanuman was so disappointed on being unable to serve Lord Rama efficiently that he wanted to end his life.

Understanding what Hanuman was going through, Lord Rama decided to give him an experiential lesson. He gently coaxed Hanuman with his sweet words. He said, 'O Hanuman, please try to understand that whatever happened has happened under a rare circumstance and is definitely not going to undermine your abilities and service to me. Sita made this Shiva Linga from sand with all her love and devotion. And you have brought this original Shiva Linga all the way from Mount Kailash after pleasing Lord Shiva. For me, both these Lingas are sacred. However, right now, you look very disturbed. So, I have decided to worship your Linga as well. Please place it below and let's begin the ritual.'

Hanuman, however, hesitated in placing it down. Studying his facial expression, Lord Rama could understand that Hanuman wasn't comfortable with the idea of his Linga being the second one. He wanted his Linga to be the only one. Lord Rama told him, 'All right, Hanuman, you remove the Linga made by Sita and replace it with yours.'

There was an instant smile on Hanuman's face. He wrapped his tail around the Shiva Linga, made by Sita using sand, and tightened his grip. Considering that it was made of sand and could crumble, he did not exert too much force. He wanted to lift it in complete shape and place it very far away. When he pulled, it didn't budge at all. He put all his might now and, still, the Linga wouldn't even move an inch. Now, Hanuman put his entire force using his hands. Yet, nothing happened. The Linga stayed!

Hanuman was frustrated; he decided to use every ounce of his energy to root out the Linga. He pulled really hard this time. With the might of Hanuman, the earth below shook but the Linga held fast. With the next heave, Hanuman lost his grip and fell off on the other side, face down. Seeing their hero collapse in this way, all the monkeys gathered around the now unconscious Hanuman. Lord Rama entered the circle, sat next to Hanuman and lovingly placed Hanuman's head on his lap. He gently ran his hands all over the exhausted body of Hanuman. Lord Rama's touch rejuvenated the disoriented hero.

He opened his eyes to the joy of all the monkeys. When he saw that he was on the lap of Lord Rama, he had tears in his eyes. Lord Rama gently stroked his head and said, 'O Hanuman, do you remember when we met first near the Pampa Lake, you had introduced me to Sugriva and had assured me that you would give us your constant support? From that day onwards, I had forgotten my father, my mother and even my brothers. You have done more than any relative would have done. I am eternally grateful for all the sacrifices you have made to serve me.'

Hearing Lord Rama's words, tears of gratitude flowed freely from Hanuman's eyes. Lord Rama, then installed the Shiva Linga brought by Hanuman close to Sita's Shiva Linga and performed the ritual again. Then he made a declaration that left everyone spellbound. He said, 'From this day on, anyone who visits Rameswaram will first worship and honour the Shiva Linga of Hanuman and only then worship Sita's Shiva Linga.'

The two Lingas stayed there, forever, announcing to the world how much Lord Rama prioritised and valued Hanuman's service.

In a competition, only one survives. However, all supporting parties survive, if they cooperate with each other.

A Motherly Anguish

'There she is!' Everyone rushed towards the direction from where the voice came. Thousands of monkeys were leaning dangerously onto the railing on one side of the Pushpaka Vimana. There were animated discussions going on. There was excitement in the air. Every monkey wanted to see her closely. Every monkey wanted to seek her blessings. Every monkey wanted to tell her that her son was great.

Her body was shining like brilliant gold. Her face was that of a monkey and her body was that of a delicate woman. Bedecked in costly ornaments, her beauty really stood out in the landscape of the greenwoods. Seated in the lotus position, with eyes closed, rapt in meditation, she was clearly an advanced yogini.

After the defeat of the Lankan army and the death of Ravana; Lord Rama along with Sita, Lakshmana and all the monkeys mounted the Pushpaka Vimana and proceeded towards Ayodhya. They stopped briefly at Kishkinda to pick the monkey ladies at the insistence of Sita. That's when Hanuman expressed his desire to see his mother and seek her blessings before proceeding further. As soon as Hanuman expressed this desire, all the monkeys seemed even more enthusiastic than him to witness this reunion.

As the Pushpaka Vimana landed on Mount Anjanadri, Hanuman jumped off and ran towards his divine mother. Falling at her feet, he began to offer his respects. Anjana was overjoyed when she saw her son lying at her feet. She instantly got up and embraced him dearly. Hanuman gently sat next to her and placed his head on her lap. She lovingly stroked his head with great affection and enquired from him about his recent adventures.

The entire monkey army sat around the mother and son, of course keeping a respectful distance and affording them a little privacy. Oblivious to the thousands of watchful eyes, Hanuman narrated all that had transpired in his life in the last five months, from the moment he met Lord Rama. He spoke excitedly about his crossing the ocean, the building of the mammoth bridge, meeting Mother Sita with Lord Rama's message, fireworks in Lanka, the eventful fight with the Lankans and the eventual killing of Ravana.

'This is nonsense!' Anjana, in great fury, rose up abruptly disrupting the flow of Hanuman's thoughts and his narration. The entire monkey army was taken aback with her anger. They retreated a few metres. Hanuman was also equally surprised at her outburst.

'You are not my worthy son! You have definitely not drunk my breast milk. I am totally disappointed by your cowardliness.' Hearing her sharp and cutting words, Hanuman was taken aback. But in spite of that, in a very humble and meek manner, he approached her and enquired the reason for her disappointment. He wasn't clear what action of his had really disappointed her so much.

Anjana then spoke her mind clearly, 'Why did you delay the complete destruction of Lanka? Didn't you have the physical strength and mental wisdom to destroy the horrible city in your very first visit itself? Why did you have to trouble Lord Rama and more than that, Sita so much? Why did the monkey army need to go through so much trouble to wage a war? You have completely disappointed me and have brought disdain to my breast milk. I disown you as my son. Go away and never return to me.'

She was breathing heavily and was really angry at her son's dismal performance. Understanding his mother's concern, Hanuman quietly kneeled at her feet and said, 'My dear mother, I wanted to do exactly that. But I had two other thoughts that prevented me from doing so. Firstly, I was sent as a messenger of Lord Rama. As a faithful servant of Lord Rama, all that was expected of me was to give Mother Sita the message and carry her message back. I wasn't told to eliminate Ravana. If I had done that, it would be tantamount to disobeying the instructions of my master. The second and more important reason that I chose to restrain myself was if I had killed Ravana myself, it would have brought infamy to Lord Rama. People would have glorified my heroism and criticised Lord Rama for being unable to protect his own wife. I wanted all the glory of the victory to go to my Lord and eternal master, Rama. I am not justifying my actions, but I am humbly submitting my thoughts for your consideration. O Mother, if you still feel I have brought you shame in any way, please tell me and I will instantly drown myself in the ocean for the sin of letting you down.'

Hearing her son's articulate explanation, Anjana was totally satisfied and embraced him lovingly. She said,

'I knew that my breast milk cannot go in vain. One who has drunk this milk could not be a coward.'

As the mother and son were absorbed in their loving embrace, Lakshmana became very uneasy and began looking here and there. There was something fishy here. Why was there so much talk about breast milk? Why was she repeatedly talking about it as if it were a rare phenomenon that babies drink their mother's milk? And what was so rare about her breast milk that she had such high expectations from Hanuman.

Anjana immediately read Lakshmana's mind. The yogini that she was, reading minds wasn't difficult. Instantly, she pulled herself from Hanuman and walked away from the army towards the rear end of the mountain. Approaching another mountain peak close by, she pressed her breast and a shower of milk shot ahead, landing on the mountain peak.

KADABOOOM!

As soon as the milk touched the mountain peak, the entire peak exploded, unable to handle the power of her milk.

The entire monkey army including Lakshmana bowed down in reverence to this divine mother who had given birth to this divine son.

Parenting is about feeding the right example.

The Private Diaries of Lord Rama

The conference took another direction when a devotee asked Hanuman a very complicated question. Hanuman tried his best to evade the question. He even changed topics several times. But this devotee insisted. Being such an exalted devotee of the Lord, Hanuman couldn't avoid facing it for long. He chose a very interesting way to answer the question without embarrassing himself by self-glorification or embarrassing that devotee by speaking the truth.

The knotty question this devotee had asked was, 'Who is the greatest devotee of the Lord today?'

Hanuman in all humility said, 'I am too small a person to say who the greatest devotee of the Lord from the galaxy of star-devotees is. But I can surely give you a clue that may help you in your quest.'

Immediately, this devotee was excited to know what Hanuman had to offer. Hanuman told him that he had heard from great saints that Lord Rama had a diary that enlisted the greatest devotees of the Lord serially. Instead of speculating, it would be best to plead with the Lord to provide access to that diary. The devotee thanked Hanuman and proceeded to meet Lord Rama.

On being requested to have a look at the diary, Lord Rama unexcitedly pointed out to the direction in which the diary was kept. This devotee approached the huge diary with great reverence and anticipation. He prayed that his name be on the list and, if possible, a little higher in rank. With great curiosity, he fingered the outer cover of the diary and admired its artwork. His lips were immersed in prayerful murmurs as he flipped open the cover of the diary to reveal its first page.

Lo and behold! His name was the first on that list. His excitement knew no bounds. With great zeal, he flipped through the scores of names in the thousands of pages that lay ahead. He was fervently searching for one name. Though he looked carefully, he just couldn't find it anywhere. He was excited that his name was there, but he was surprised that the other name wasn't there. With half-excitement and half-worry, he ran back to Hanuman to share his findings and concerns.

'Hanuman, I have a good and bad news. The good news is my name was on the Lord's list and it was the first name in the Lord's diary.' Then, with a sad face, he continued, 'But the bad news is your name was not there. I meticulously searched the entire diary trying to find your name. But I am sorry to say that it wasn't there. I am sure there must be some mistake. You are such a wonderful devotee. How could the Lord miss your name?'

Hanuman smiled at the struggle of this devotee to convey the message. He then asked a question that threw this devotee completely off guard. He asked, 'Did you check the small diary of Lord Rama?'

'What! Lord Rama has another diary? He didn't tell me about that. Are you sure…' Completely confused, this devotee didn't even wait for Hanuman to reply to his question. He rushed back to Lord Rama. Lord Rama was surprised at his quick return. Falling at Lord Rama's feet, the devotee asked the Lord if he had another smaller diary.

With a big smile on his moon-like face, Lord Rama reached out to his inner pocket close to his heart and gracefully removed a small dairy. He held it gently as if it were a precious and rare commodity. Hesitatingly, he handed it over to this devotee. Comparing the mood of Lord Rama in giving him access to both the diaries, this devotee could understand there was something special about this particular diary. With a puzzled mind and trembling hands, he thumbed the diary and slowly opened it.

To his surprise and shock, the first name was that of Hanuman. His eagerness and desperation grew by the second, as he couldn't find his name on any page of this diary. Overwhelmed with emotion and gripped with confusion, this devotee fell at the Lord's feet and requested for an explanation about the two diaries he had seen. Lord Rama's explanation revealed the essence of true devotion.

He said, 'The first diary contains the names of all those devotees who constantly strive to remember me. The second diary contains the names of all those devotees whom I strive to constantly remember.'

Tears flowed incessantly from this devotee's eyes as he ran from Lord Rama's abode to that of Hanuman. He fell at the feet of Hanuman who gently picked him and embraced him. What was the need to know the name of the greatest devotee? The need was to act in such an exemplary way that the Lord strives to remember you.

Impressing the mind is a public affair and winning hearts is a private affair.

The Red Monkey

For a second, Sita wondered why Hanuman followed her everywhere today. But in the next moment, she brushed aside that thought. She was convinced of his innocence. Though he had a gigantic body, he had a childlike innocence. Sometimes, she wondered if people took undue advantage of his innocence.

She continued with her activities without bothering about Hanuman's inquisitive presence. She was preparing for Lord Rama's return from the court. Sitting in front of a huge ornate mirror, she took a pinch of red vermilion in her fingers and raised it to the parting of her hair. Deftly, she placed it right in the middle and drew a short red line along the parting, rubbing the powder neatly.

Unable to understand, Hanuman stared quizzically. He began to walk closer to her and continued staring at the vermilion mark in the parting of her hair. He finally spoke, 'What's that? What is that red mark?'

Sita giggled at his innocence. She was surprised to know that Hanuman was so naïve about worldly things. He seemed to have no idea about the customs of this world. He didn't even know the reason why a married woman, in the Vedic tradition, puts vermilion in the parting of her hair. The red mark indicated that she was married. She decided there was no point in explaining the details to a person who was so simple. Only the essence would be enough to satisfy the inquisitive Hanuman.

'This red mark pleases Lord Rama! That's why I wear it.' Sita nonchalantly replied and continued her dressing ritual.

Everything froze for Hanuman at this point. Her words kept ringing in his ears. He had got what he had been looking for. His effort had been worth it. All day, he had been patiently hovering around Sita, looking for a clue on how she managed to please Lord Rama. And she had revealed her secret.

He ran out of Sita's palace and went into the streets of Ayodhya. He was in such haste that people had to step aside to avoid bumping into him. He ran at great speed through the market places of Ayodhya, stopping only when he reached his destination. This was the warehouse of a cloth merchant. Seeing the respectable hero, Hanuman, walk into their abode, the merchant got up to receive him. But Hanuman brushed him aside, ignoring the formalities and barged into his warehouse. The merchant was stunned at his behaviour.

Suddenly, a heavy splash was heard followed by a gurgling sound of water. No one knew what was happening. The next moment, all the workers in the warehouse began giggling. Soon, they started laughing. They were rolling on the ground, holding their tummies, trying to control their laughter.

A red monkey was standing in front of them. It was obvious that Hanuman had jumped into a vat of red-coloured water dye. He was bathed in red from head to toe. No one could understand what was on his mind. They only found the scene very funny.

Leaving the warehouse, Hanuman began to walk on the streets of Ayodhya. With red dye dripping from his body, he was leaving a reddish trail as he walked. Peals of laughter echoed through the streets of Ayodhya when the citizens recognised the walking red monkey. They couldn't believe what Hanuman had done to himself. Hanuman ignored all the fun people were making of him and focussed on his goal.

Soon, he entered the royal courtroom of Lord Rama. There was a serious conference going on. Suddenly, Lord Rama began to chuckle. Everyone was taken aback. Why was he chuckling in the middle of such an important discussion? By then, Lord Rama had begun to laugh heartily. He was rolling sideways on his throne, trying to control his laughter. The courtiers couldn't understand why the otherwise serious King was laughing so much. Suddenly, one of them joined Lord Rama in his laughter and with difficulty told the others, 'Look who is here! A red monkey!'

Everyone in the courtroom began laughing their guts out. What confused them the most was that the happiest amongst them seemed Hanuman.

Lord Rama managed to control his laughter and finally asked him, 'Can we know what is the secret behind this new look of yours, Hanuman?'

Hanuman smiled brilliantly and said, 'My Lord, for many days, I have been spying on Mother Sita to find out exactly what is it about her that pleases you so much. And finally, I tricked her into giving out the secret. When she was dressing up, she told me that the red mark on her forehead pleases you the most. Immediately, I concluded that if a little red mark could please you so much, surely you would be pleased beyond imagination if I covered myself completely in red. And as soon as I entered the courtroom today, I got my proof that the idea really worked. I have never seen you so happy in my life. I have never seen you laugh so much. The success of my life is to bring you happiness. I have found the magic formula for making you happy. A red monkey!'

Innocence adds beauty to strength.

What a Deal!

Somewhere in the royal palaces of Ayodhya, a secret conference was taking place. Every important person closely connected to the royal family was there, except one. All precautions had been taken to ensure that the person doesn't even get a hint of this conference and its proceedings. It was an intense discussion. The only agenda of this conference was one word—service!

Once the conference was over, a list was drafted on a velvety cloth and embossed in gold ink. The final approval had to come from the King. There was an air of nervousness in the room. Would the idealistic King approve of their decision? Some were tapping their fingers on the armrests of their ivory seats. Others were tapping their foot on the gems-studded marble floor. Some were watching the door to make sure that person didn't come before the King took his decision.

After a lot of thought, Lord Rama spoke, his eyebrows arched giving him the look of a thinker. 'I approve!'

Instantly, the tension eased and everyone jumped up on their seats and embraced one another. They were now ready to carry out their new roles. The list had the names of each one of them who were assembled and the service they were going to offer to Lord Rama from now on. The team had made sure that they had enlisted every possible service that Lord Rama would need and had allotted a name to carry out each responsibility. Now, everyone had their own personal service to Lord Rama. All, except one!

That's exactly when he entered! He had realised that something fishy was going on in Ayodhya. He had been sent on an urgent errand which was actually a hoax. He knew there was something cooking in his absence. As soon as he entered the court and saw the celebration, he immediately put two and two together and deciphered the riddle. The letter in the hands of Lord Rama was proof of his thought process.

For the last few weeks in Ayodhya, everyone was dissatisfied with the fact that he was doing every service possible for Lord Rama. In his presence, no one got a chance to do anything. Many had voiced their dissatisfaction openly. He couldn't fathom what was wrong with his actions. He was only trying his best to serve Lord Rama. And if his best meant no opportunity for others, what could he do? How was he to be blamed?

Anyway, the others had had their way now. They had managed to convince Lord Rama to approve a list of services and had clearly allotted those amongst themselves, which simply meant there was nothing left for him to do for Lord Rama. There was only one way out of this—get the list.

Cool as a cucumber, he strolled towards Lord Rama's throne. The celebrations had now come to an end. All eyes were glued on him. Lord Rama gave him a knowing smile. He held out his hands and without any exchange of words, Lord Rama handed over the list to him. When that happened, everyone gasped! Oh no! All their efforts could get spoiled in a moment. No doubt they had made sure to keep everything watertight and no service however minor had been missed. But with him around, you never knew. In the next few minutes there was pin-drop silence as he scrutinised the list. Nervousness was all around!

'Aha!' Everyone jolted at his sudden surcharge of excitement. 'I got it!'

Lord Rama was still smiling at the group's dynamics. He never liked anyone sidelining anyone else or anyone usurping everything himself. There had to be sensitivity and cooperation in service. He said, 'Yes, Hanuman. Please tell me what your observation is.'

'There is one service that is not mentioned in this list. Would you allow me to perform that one at least?' Hanuman looked at Lord Rama pleadingly. There was no point in looking at the others, as none of them would have sympathised with him. Lord Rama nodded his head to the dismay of all others. 'Please tell us which service is missing from this list?'

With the innocent smile of a child, Hanuman said, 'Snapping!'

What! No one could decipher what Hanuman meant. They gazed at him quizzically. He explained, enjoying himself thoroughly at their helplessness. 'You see when Lord Rama yawns, there has to be someone who will snap his fingers in front of his mouth. With the Lord's permission, I would like to take up this small service while all of you execute the big services.'

Hearing his idea, everyone smiled. They hadn't expected him to be so foolish. Lord Rama hardly ever yawned. They were only too happy to consent to this proposal. It wasn't going to affect them in anyway and it effectively meant that Hanuman would have nothing to do. Everyone dispersed to immerse themselves in their own services while Hanuman continued to stand next to Lord Rama, eagerly waiting for him to yawn.

All day, he kept staring at Lord Rama, not wanting to miss out a single yawn, even if it was a small one. Once it was evening and the court proceedings were completed, Lord Rama left the courtroom and proceeded to his private quarters to spend time with Sita. Sita had been eagerly waiting for his return to her inner chambers to spend some private, loving moments with him. She really longed for those days they had spent in the woods amidst undisturbed and uninterrupted love. Anyway, now she had learnt to be content with the little time she got to spend with him after dusk.

As soon as Lord Rama entered her bedroom, her heart fluttered with joy. She ran up to him to embrace him lovingly. Just as she was about to take him into her arms, she shrieked! 'What's this? What is he doing here?' Behind Lord Rama stood Hanuman with his hands folded behind his back and a naughty smile on his face.

Angrily, she said, 'What are you doing here, Hanuman? Don't you know this is our private time?'

Hanuman spoke smilingly, 'My dear mother, I am only following the decision that was taken in the court today, right in your presence. I have been given the only service of snapping when Lord Rama yawns. And that, he can do at any time. Even if he yawns in his sleep, wouldn't it be time for my snapping duty?'

Sita was resigned to her fate, hearing his logic. All night, Hanuman sat right in front of Lord Rama gazing lovingly at his beautiful face and Sita regretted the decision of the court.

The next morning, there was a conference again. This time, no one was missing from the conference. Another list was made. Of course, there was one item deleted from this list. The snap deal!

Cooperation is the gift that followers give to reciprocate with a leader's vision.

Chained to Liberate

'When death becomes a protector, who will be his destroyer?'
This was the only question the entire army of Lord Rama
asked that day. They were engaged in a gruesome war with
the army of King Surat. He was the King of Kundalpura.
The sacrificial horse of Lord Rama had entered his territory
that morning and had been captured by Champaka, the
brave son of King Surat.

Lord Rama's army appointed Angad to negotiate before
declaring war. Angad's negotiation skills were well known
from the time of the war. Despite using all his persuasion
skills, Angad could not manage to convince the King
to release the horse. While Angad was returning from
the palace dejected and angry, he overheard two sepoys
discussing their King. He couldn't clearly hear everything,
but what he heard shocked him! They were talking about
their King being immortal due to some benediction given
to him by the God of Death. Since they were walking away
from Angad, their voices were getting progressively faint.
But he did manage to catch a few more words... 'If Lord
Rama comes...'

What did that mean? How could a mere human being be immortal? How could the God of Death grant such a boon to a mere local King? With confusion in his head and anger in his heart, Angad returned and immediately a war was declared. Initially, only a chunk of the armies went into combat. Lord Rama's army was led by Pushkala, the son of Bharata and King Surat's army was under the guidance of Champaka. Though Pushkala fought fiercely, he was no match to Champaka and the former lost piteously.

This time, Hanuman decided to go as a messenger. Despite offering innumerable explanations, King Surat was unrelenting in returning the horse peacefully. Hanuman realised—from his experience—that there had to be a clear reasoning for this otherwise pious King's adamant behaviour. He acted as if he had left the palace in disgust. But, he returned in a very small form to learn more about the King's mindset. When he returned, he heard the King talking to his son with tears in his eyes.

He said, 'This horse is the harbinger of my liberation. I was told by Yamaraj that I will not leave this body, until Lord Rama himself personally comes to my abode to liberate me from the clutches of birth and death. The only reason Lord Rama will come to this wretched place is if his devotees are in great trouble. Though I do not want to trouble the Lord's devotees who are my venerable masters, I have no choice but to do it. In front of them, I may act adamant, but in reality, I only cry tears of repentance for having troubled my masters for my own selfish liberation.'

After learning the truth, Hanuman decided to intervene in this matter himself. The next day, Hanuman himself led the troops to war. When news came that Hanuman was leading, King Surat himself rallied his troops. The fight began intensely, with both sides causing casualties with all the force they could muster. Soon, the fight took an unprecedented turn when King Surat managed to tie Hanuman with ropes. As soon as Hanuman was tied, everyone stopped fighting. King Surat laughed at the top of his voice and held his sword close to the neck of Hanuman. The entire army of Lord Rama was flabbergasted at the turn of events. They couldn't believe that their superhero had been tied up in such an ordinary way by an insignificant and powerless King. But, none of them could do anything, lest any harm be caused to Hanuman.

Hanuman closed his eyes and earnestly began to chant the names of Lord Rama, 'Rama…Rama…Rama…' The vibrations of Lord Rama's holy names chanted by Hanuman began to ascend in all directions and soon, the entire area was filled with the potent vibrations of his chant.

Suddenly, conches began to blow and in a flash, Lord Rama appeared in front of Hanuman with a pleasant smile on his lotus face. With the appearance of Lord Rama, the ropes of Hanuman's bondage fell at his feet. As soon as he saw Lord Rama, King Surat fell to the ground like a stick offering his obeisance. His body began to tremble in ecstasy and tears began to flow profusely from his eyes.

Seeing the King's elevated state of consciousness, Hanuman beamed, thinking it was worth it to be tied for some time to allow another to be liberated forever.

On the face of helplessness, sometimes, a mask of haughtiness is worn.

An Enlightening Kick

A 16-year-old lad had captured the Ashwamedha horse, surprising the leaders of Lord Rama's entourage. Though very young, his self-confidence was sky high. He blew his conch loudly and in turn, hundreds of conches blew in reciprocation. Soon, Lord Rama's army, led by Shatrughna, was surrounded in three directions by the army of the Chitranga kingdom.

Damana, the first son of Subahu, the King of Chitranga, was still holding the horse and glaring fiercely at the enemies. Damana was clearly in charge of this fight. Shatrughna and his army were surprised with the immense valour exhibited by this boy. At this point, Pushkala, the son of Bharata, stepped ahead to lead the army. After a passionate fight, Pushkala rendered Damana unconscious. Damana's shrewd and agile chariot driver whisked him off to safety.

After Damana's departure, the King of Chitranga, Subahu appeared on the scene along with his brother Suketu. The King's arrival filled the army of Chitranga with a renewed burst of energy. They attacked with full fury. Slowly, Shatrughna's army started collapsing. Suketu, especially, proved destructive. With his free-swinging double maces, he was violently disabling thousands of soldiers.

King Subahu's second son, Chitranga (who was named after the kingdom) joined the war. He had been thus far busy transporting the unconscious Damana to safety. As soon as he made his entry, he wreaked havoc in Lord Rama's army. Realising the chaos that this youngster was creating, Pushkala entered and challenged Chitranga. Soon, Chitranga's head was seen rolling on the battlefield.

The death of his son aggrieved King Subahu. He went mad with rage and began slaughtering whoever came in his vicinity. To stop the mass destruction the maddened King was causing, Hanuman came and stood in front of the King, blocking access to the army. King Subahu began shooting arrows at Hanuman rapidly. Hanuman caught every arrow and broke it. Suddenly, King Subahu felt his chariot going a bit wobbly. Next, the chariot began to quake. He dropped his bow to hold on to the railings of the chariot. That's when he realised that his chariot was being air-lifted. He couldn't understand who was lifting the chariot. When the chariot was sufficiently high, he could see from one corner that Hanuman had coiled his tail around the chariot and had raised it up.

Hanuman also began to fly and reached the same level as the chariot. Now, the King had recovered his stability and resumed shooting arrows at Hanuman, aiming at the Monkey God's chest. The arrows found their mark, and Hanuman was badly injured. This enraged Hanuman so much that he flew towards the King and kicked him hard on his chest. The kick was so powerful that the King toppled over his chariot and fell with a thud on the ground. The kick and the fall left the King dazed. His head began to spin and his mind was all muddled up.

Suddenly, King Subahu saw a brilliant flash of light in front of him. This light seemed almost ethereal. The war that was going on didn't matter anymore. He felt as if he had been transported to another realm. There was another green flash and in front of his eyes stood Lord Rama in full glory. He was smiling and was blessing him with raised hands. Tears began to well up in the King's eyes. He fell on his knees and folded his palms in supplication and bowed down to the Lord. The next instant, the vision vanished, to be replaced by the gruesome battle.

King Subahu ran frantically to his brother and his army men, asking them to stop fighting. With the King desperate to stop the fight, the soldiers laid down their weapons and the war ceased. His brother wanted to know the reason for his sudden change of mind. King Subahu spoke something that surprised everyone, particularly Lord Rama's army men.

He narrated a story on what had happened in his life many years back. 'I once visited a sage named Atisanga to gain knowledge about the higher truths of life. His only advice to me was to take shelter at Lord Rama's feet and chant his holy names. Of course at that point, I couldn't perceive Lord Rama to be anything other than an earthly King. I wasn't able to comprehend how he could be God. I challenged the sage using logic. Because I doubted the truth, the sage pronounced a curse—that I would never be able to achieve knowledge of the higher truths of life, and would spend this life only filling up my belly.

'I was saddened to hear this curse. I fell at his feet, beseeching kindness. His heart melted seeing my sincerity and he declared that the higher truths would be mystically revealed to me the day the sacrificial horse of Lord Rama would be captured by my men and I would receive a kick from

Hanuman. The divine knowledge possessed by Hanuman was transmitted to me by a mere kick. I was fortunate enough to have Lord Rama's darshan, right here on this battlefield. With one kick, Hanuman has kicked away my ignorance forever and filled my heart with love for Lord Rama.'

King Subahu fell at the feet of Hanuman and every other person in the army of Lord Rama. This was the kick-start to a life of devotion!

Often, wisdom gets kicked into our life through an experience.

The Frozen Horse

The entourage had been passing through thousands of towns, villages and cities. Hundreds of mountains were scaled, numerous rivers crossed, tons of battles won, scores of rulers subjugated and a kingdom won. The tour was definitely a grand success. Until a problem arose that was not just weird, but was crazily weird.

The sacrificial horse that they were following around the world had frozen!

Right in the middle of its trot, it froze. One of its front legs was raised up as if it was going to move ahead. But it just stood there, transfixed. Even its eyes didn't blink any more. Its tail which was earlier flapping around, now remained frozen mid-air.

Hanuman was the first to reach the spot to inspect the frozen horse. He touched its body and it was still warm. Other than that, the horse had become a statue. He tried coaxing it, but it did not move. There was no response.

Much after the coronation of Lord Rama as the King of Ayodhya, an Ashwamedha Yajna had been organised. This was the horse that was chosen for the sacrifice. Before beginning such a yajna, the King had to prove his supremacy across the globe. The horse had already travelled more than half the globe. With powerful warriors like Hanuman, Shatrughna, Pushkala around, they were on the threshold of victory. Any King who challenged the progress of the horse was thwarted by the combined powers of these super-warriors.

But now, the combined strength of these heroes was useless. Even their combined intelligence proved futile. Try as they did to make the horse move, they were sorely unsuccessful. In fact, they even tried raising the horse using a crane. The horse had become so heavy that they couldn't lift it either. Not even Hanuman's mountainous strength was of any help that day.

'I have seen that whenever Lord Rama comes across a problem that he has no solution for, he consults the wisdom of the sages. Let's find a sage who can guide us to crack this enigma.' Hanuman spoke after much deliberation.

With a little enquiry, they came across Sage Shaunaka. They discussed the problem and requested the sage for a solution. Instead of replying to them, the sage closed his eyes. They didn't know what to make of it. They waited for a while. With no response, they started retreating. Just then, they heard a voice.

'HMMMM….'

What did that mean? They turned to see the sage open his eyes while his mind still meditated on some deep mystery. They fell on their knees to hear what the sage had to say. 'This is the doing of a brahma rakshasa (demon). Many years back, a brahmin had messed around with a few sages. The sages angrily cursed him to become a demon. Knowing the implication of such a curse, the brahmin fell at their feet and begged for redemption. Considering his ardent appeal, they offered him a conditional redemption. They told him that he would be relieved of his curse if he ever got the opportunity to hear Rama Katha. And of course they also foretold that such an occasion would come the day the sacrificial horse of Lord Rama would enter his life.'

The sage retreated into a trance, leaving the group with a valuable clue to solve their dilemma. They returned and assembled around the stranded horse. Hanuman sat down on a flat piece of rock in the lotus posture and closed his eyes. Thoughts began to inundate the banks of his mind. He began to recall the entire life story of Lord Rama.

In an enchantingly melodious voice, Hanuman began to sing the Ramayana. He narrated every episode with emotion and complete details. With each section of the story of Lord Rama being narrated, different parts of the horse began to move. As soon as Hanuman finished the narration of the heroic deeds of Lord Rama, the horse was completely agile and relieved.

Suddenly, a huge branch of a Banyan tree cracked and fell on the ground with a massive thud. The brahma rakshasa was liberated too. Flowers began to shower on Hanuman, indicating an auspicious culmination of an inauspicious event.

Being wrongly overactive forces one to be helplessly inactive.
Both wrong action and inaction are by-products of ignorance.
Only auspicious action is the by-product of knowledge.

Lord Rama's Powerless Arrows

'Why did Narada ask me to do such a terrible thing?' The King of Kashi came out of Lord Rama's courtroom completely confused. He was constantly cursing himself for following Narada's advice. On the one hand, he knew that the advice of great and saintly people is always for one's uplift; on the other hand, he couldn't fathom how he could be uplifted after enraging Lord Rama so much.

What was done was done. All he needed at this point of time was an idea to save his life from the arrows of Lord Rama. As soon as Lord Rama said that he would cut off his head by that evening, he began to run frantically. His mind raced faster than his legs. Probably for the first time, he was thinking while running. After a lot of thinking, he concluded that the only person who could help him under this dire circumstance was the very person who got him in trouble in the first place. There must be some reason why the sage had given him that advice and he would surely have a counter measure for the impending catastrophe.

Falling at the feet of Narada, the King of Kashi said, 'O Narada Muni! O Divine Sage! I am in deep trouble! My only sin is that I followed your instructions perfectly.

You instructed me to visit Lord Rama and pay my respects only to him, completely neglecting the others present there. I did just that. Unfortunately, I didn't notice that the angry Sage Vishwamitra was also present in the assembly. Naturally, due to my ignorance and my wish to be loyal to your instructions, I did not pay my respects to him as well. That neglect flared up his anger and he expressed his dissatisfaction at my conduct towards Lord Rama. Instantly, Lord Rama pronounced the decision that he would behead me by this evening. He even selected three arrows from his quiver for this purpose. Now, O Narada Muni, I am totally dependent on you. Save me from Lord Rama's wrath!'

Narada had a naughty smile on his face. It almost seemed as though he had expected this outcome from his instructions. He said, 'O King, have faith in me. Just follow my instructions and something special will be revealed to the world this evening through you. At once, go to Anjana, the mother of Hanuman; if there is anyone who can protect you today, it is she.'

The King of Kashi ran to Anjana's abode at once and fell at her feet in desperation. Anjana called upon her able son Hanuman and instructed him to protect the fearful King's life. Hanuman accompanied the petrified King to the banks of River Sarayu. There, he asked the King to immerse himself neck-deep in the waters of the river and begin chanting the names of Lord Rama and Sita uninterruptedly. Thus began the King of Kashi's waiting period…

The first arrow came after a couple of hours. The sound of that arrow was deafening. Though his eyes were closed, the King heard the sound. He realised his death was near. He chanted Lord Rama's holy names even more intensely. The King's army was stationed at the riverbank. When they saw the arrow rushing towards their King, they all lifted their weapons to protect their beloved King, but could hardly do anything to stop it. All eyes turned towards sankata mochana (protector) Hanuman.

Hanuman had stationed himself close to the meditating King. The arrow came rushing at great speed. As it reached the throat of the King, Hanuman, placing his mouth adjacent to the King's throat, chanted, 'R..A..M..A'. He had timed it to such perfection that just when the arrow reached close to the throat, the vibrations of the holy names of Lord Rama hit the arrow, and the arrow was neatly deflected and fell to the ground.

In the next few minutes, another arrow came. It met with the same result! When the third arrow arrived, Hanuman decided to receive it with more respect. He stood right in front of the King chanting the holy names of Lord Rama. The arrow came whizzing and straightaway hit the chest of Hanuman with great force. Everyone was shocked to see that. As soon as the arrow hit the chest of Hanuman, it transformed into a beautiful lotus garland adorning his chest.

When Lord Rama realised that his arrows were being diverted by some force and not being able to hit the target, he sent Lakshmana to verify the ground situation. He wanted to know who had the impudence of foiling his attempts at disciplining a wrongdoer. After his survey, when Lakshmana reported to Lord Rama that Hanuman was behind the whole thing, Lord Rama summoned Hanuman in great anger. Hanuman was the last person Lord Rama had expected this kind of audacity from. Stopping Lord Rama's arrow from reaching its mark was not an ordinary offence!

Hanuman entered Lord Rama's court in his usual meek and humble demeanour. This angered Lord Rama further. 'This is hypocrisy! You show your humility here and elsewhere your haughtiness. Why did you meddle around with my punishment?'

Hanuman retained his humble demeanour and addressed Lord Rama, 'My Lord, I was only following your instructions. You had once told me that whoever chants your holy names, it's my duty to personally protect that person. That's exactly what I was doing. When your arrows reached the King of Kashi, he was helplessly and intensely chanting your holy names. What else am I supposed to do other than protect him? If I didn't protect him, your holy names would have been rendered ineffective and if I did protect him, your arrow would have been rendered ineffective. I felt that protecting the effectiveness of your potent holy names was far more important.'

Lord Rama was very pleased with Hanuman's answer, but he couldn't possibly smile or express his happiness openly because Sage Vishwamitra was still furious. As Lord Rama was pondering over this dilemma, Narada expertly sent the King of Kashi to fall at the feet of Sage Vishwamitra and instructed him to ask for forgiveness. Having forgiven him, Sage Vishwamitra came to the court and declared that he had forgiven the King and there was no need to punish him anymore.

Lord Rama heaved a sigh of relief. All's well that ends well!

Just like pressure applied from two directions results in a finely ground powder, contradictions created by two independently thoughtful personalities result in finely grounded learning.

A Quarrel with Shani

Seated on a mountain, Hanuman was reminiscing the most exciting project of his life. A project that still gave him goosebumps—building a 100-yojana long and 10-yojana wide bridge in five days flat. Unheard of! It was all possible because of Lord Rama. Everyone, even those who were not expected to be involved in the project, worked at least a thousand times their capacity. So many heads, so many hands, but one goal—to please Lord Rama. Love can make one do anything. The proof was the bridge.

With these exalted thoughts, Hanuman opened his eyes to glance at the remnants of the bridge he was instrumental in building thousands of years ago. He was greeted by a surprise. A dark, mammoth figure was looming over him menacingly. It was subtle...very subtle. The weak-hearted would have panicked. But Hanuman smiled. His smile was subtler. Knowledge helps one smile in the midst of perceived crisis.

'O old monkey, your time of heroism is up! It's my reign now!' In an arrogantly threatening voice, Shani, the demigod in-charge of Saturn spoke, glaring at Hanuman. Hanuman was not interested at all. At this age, he wanted to only focus on his spiritual practice. He had dealt with enough arrogant fools in his younger days to get provoked. 'You are right! I agree. Now, let me focus on my Lord.' Hanuman then closed his eyes.

'You foolish monkey! Just because you saved me when I was caught by Ravana doesn't mean I can't challenge you. I thanked you that time for your help and that event is history. Now I want to prove to the world that my might is greater than yours. Get up and put up a fight. Don't retire like a coward.' Shani began to tug at Hanuman's arms. As he tried to pull him up with a jerk, something happened... something that didn't fit into his plan.

Hanuman's tail began to coil around Shani's feet. As Hanuman tightened the grip, Shani's feet were brought together forcibly. The tail then coiled around his entire body, all the way till his chest. Shani was rendered totally helpless. He couldn't budge an inch.

Suddenly, Hanuman leapt up in the air. He began to fly, dragging an embarrassed Shani along with him. He flew towards the vast expanse of the ocean. Shani was in panic mode now, being tossed around at great speed. Then Hanuman came down at a lower altitude, flying close to the surface of the ocean. Unexpectedly, the tail flapped and thrust Shani into the ocean. A scream was heard. He plunged face down into the ocean. His head hit something very hard—a stone that was floating in the middle of the ocean, and began to bleed. Realisation dawned on him that once upon a time, this stone was a part of Lord Rama's bridge. Just as this thought crossed his mind, his head cracked again. Hanuman was beating him systematically on every stone of the bridge that still existed. The pain was excruciating. Shani was going mad with pain. But his hands and legs were tied with Hanuman's strong tail. The speed at which things were happening made him dizzy.

He closed his eyes and prepared to expect the worse. Just then, the tail began to uncoil and released him. He fell with a thud. They were back on the same mountain where the ordeal had begun.

'So, what were you saying, Shani? Was it something about strength or was it something about being a coward?' Hanuman enquired, feigning innocence. 'I had to take a look at the bridge I helped in getting built. Sorry, I interrupted your thought flow. What exactly did you want from me?'

Shani was still recovering from the 'joy' ride he had been on. While his body was still reeling, his pride was intact. He spoke, 'I was saying that the age of Kali has started with the departure of Krishna from this Earth. In this age, my influence will be the strongest. You may physically be stronger than me, but only I can influence at the level of the mind. I have come to warn you that you should leave this planet and reside elsewhere. I will dominate Earth now. I am allowed to influence every human being on Earth for seven-and-a-half years once in every 22-and-a-half years.'

Hanuman told him that he was not a human being but a celestial and couldn't be influenced by his tyranny in any way. Shani argued that anyone who had lived in the earthly realm, whoever he may be, would have to be under his subjugation for some length of time. And he added that his favourite people were the elderly nearing death. Hanuman was irritated by his haughtiness.

He asked, 'How do you influence people, could you kindly explain?'

Shani delivered a prepared speech to answer his question. 'I follow a regular procedure for breaking people. I divide the seven-and-a-half years into three parts to ensure complete destruction of an individual at every level. During the first two-and-a-half year period, I reside in their head and work on the mental faculty of the individual. I mess up their mind. I make them misunderstand others' intentions and misinterpret events and situations. Once they get mentally messed up, the next two-and-a-half years, I muddle up their gastrointestinal tract by residing there. A bad stomach is the cause of all deadly diseases. By messing with it, I put them in an endless loop of ailments. And the last two-and-a-half years, I make them wander around pointlessly by residing in their feet and spending all their money. At the end of seven-and-half years of my influence, a person turns into a totally messed-up person.'

Hanuman seemed impressed. He shrugged his shoulders and said, 'You seem to become very powerful once you enter the body.'

Shani said, 'Since you have decided to fight me, let me show you what I can do to you.'

Shani quickly entered Hanuman's head and gave him a terrible headache. Hanuman silently walked up to a nearby mountain, lifted it and placed it on his head. Shani suddenly felt a great load on his back. He began to scream from within Hanuman's head. Hanuman next lifted another mountain and placed it over the first. The pressure on Shani's back began to mount. Hanuman kept adding more and more mountains and walked around balancing them on his head. By now, there were four mountains, one over the other on his head. With so much weight, Hanuman did not feel anything. But Shani was suffering intensely.

He begged Hanuman when he saw him walking towards another mountain. 'Please remove the mountains from your head. The pressure is unbearable for me. I am dying. Please, I beg of you. I will only stay in your body for two-and-half days. Please relieve me of this burden.'

This deal didn't satisfy Hanuman. He walked further towards another mountain. Just as he lifted a fifth mountain to place on his head, Shani screamed at the top of his lungs. 'PLEASE…DON'T KILL ME! I beg you. I will never ever trouble you again. I will never even bother anyone who takes your name. PLEASE LET ME GO…'

Realising that his pride had been totally crushed, Hanuman shrugged off the mountains from his head and Shani came staggering out of his head. In pain, he was holding on to his back with both hands. Every limb of his body was throbbing. Crashing on his knees in front of Hanuman, he begged for some massage oil to relieve him of his pain.

'I am a recluse, where will I get oil from? Why don't you beg those people whom you trouble, for some oil?' And Hanuman walked away.

From that day on, people regularly pour oil over his aching limbs to help him, but they end up reminding him of this ordeal. And from that day, Shani kept his promise too, lest, the tail of Hanuman comes crawling down…

Embarrassment is the fee you pay for playing mental games with a stronger mind.

The Divine Monkey Missile

'It's an attack on Mathura!' The citizens started to panic.

Without any announcement, a terrible missile had attacked the city, creating havoc. There was mayhem everywhere. The army was alerted instantly. The warning bells were sounded and everyone was commanded to be vigilant within their homes or rush to the nearest palace for shelter.

Amidst this chaos, Krishna's sons got together for a quick discussion on how to bring the situation under control. The onus of protecting Mathura was on them since both, their father Krishna and uncle Balarama were away. Considering this a test of their martial abilities, they decided to give it their best shot. They vowed to protect each other under all circumstances and so, vowed to not retreat at any cost.

The gigantic doors of the fort were thrown open. The bloodthirsty Yadava army, rallied by the young princes, charged out in a frenzy but quickly froze in their tracks. What's this? How can this be possible!

In front of them was an army of 10,000 soldiers. But, that was immaterial. The surprise element was right ahead, leading the attack. It was this unbelievably huge demon named Kalanka. He was so huge that the soldier sitting on the elephant was only reaching up to his knee. His ferocious looks accentuated the terror among the soldiers. The Yadavas had no idea how to counteract such an enemy. Everyone sorely missed Krishna's presence in their midst.

Kalanka was quick to begin the assault. He bent down and picked up soldiers, chariots, and elephants alike. At his mere touch, the animals cried piteously. When he squeezed them through his fingers, they bled profusely. Shockingly, he picked them up and directly put them into his mouth! The Yadavas were terrified and the leaders were helpless.

Krishna's sons began to shoot arrows at him from all directions. He wasn't even concerned about the arrows, let alone being hurt by them. Finally, one of Krishna's sons shot a divine missile, the Kapindastra or the monkey missile. As soon as the Kapindastra was fired, a monkey appeared on the war-field. In a flash, the monkey grew in size and assumed the regal form of Hanuman.

In a few seconds, Hanuman had grown to match the size of Kalanka. He stood right in front of Kalanka with his hands on his hips. Kalanka plunged to grab Hanuman, but Hanuman ducked in time, throwing the demon off balance. Then, Hanuman grabbed Kalanka by his hips and lifted him in the air well above his head. Effortlessly, he threw the terrible demon in the sky like a small child throws a ball. The demon was flabbergasted by Hanuman's power. While the demon was falling headlong, he threw a club with great force at Hanuman. Hanuman ducked the club and it crashed against the wall of the fort of Mathura, smashing the wall to powder. Meanwhile, Hanuman held up his fist in such a way that he hit Kalanka square on his jaws as he landed on the ground. Kalanka fell half dead.

Hanuman jumped over the semi-conscious Kalanka and returned in a few seconds, with a huge mountain. He dropped it flat on Kalanka, squashing him under the mountain's weight. Thus ended the terror of Kalanka, he was safely buried under the mountain of his own pride.

Relationships struggle to survive when squashed under the mountain of pride.

The Bridge of Arrows

The screams of Draupadi were still fresh in his mind. Though she had five capable husbands, she had to undergo many traumatic experiences in her life—that too, not by strangers, but her own relatives. Jayadratha had crossed all limits when he attempted to kidnap her in their absence. Though Arjuna and Bhima had managed to track him on time and rescue her, the ordeal had shaken all of them up. Arjuna, in particular, was deeply affected. He needed someone to pacify his reeling mind. He ventured out looking for someone who could apply the salve of tender wisdom to his hurt mind.

He found Rishi Markendeya near a river, as if by providence. The Rishi heard his sorrowful tale and pacified him by narrating the story of the Ramayana, where Lord Rama had to suffer a similar and more complicated anguish when Ravana kidnapped his wife Sita. Lord Rama had to take the help of the monkey army and construct a stone bridge across the ocean to fight Ravana and rescue his wife. Hearing this tale, Arjuna did seem pacified, but what troubled his mind most was the story of Lord Rama and the monkey army building the stone bridge.

Nearby, Hanuman was meditating and chanting the holy names of Lord Rama. Hanuman was aware of Arjuna's restlessness. He instantly took the form of an old monkey and proceeded towards Arjuna. Rishi Markendeya had already left and Arjuna was standing on the banks of the river and wondering about Lord Rama's competence as an archer. He may be a great person, but was he really as great an archer as Krishna and Bhishma claimed he was?

The old monkey came and stood next to Arjuna. He spoke as if he could read Arjuna's thoughts. 'In those days, monkeys were really strong and powerful. A bridge of arrows could never have withstood their weight and might.'

For a moment, Arjuna was surprised at how this old monkey could decipher his inner thoughts. But his spirit to prove his point carried him away. 'The hallmark of a good archer is the ability to do anything and everything with his arrows. If Lord Rama was indeed a master archer, he should have built the bridge with his arrows rather than rely on the monkey army for the task. More than anything else, the task could have been accomplished in minutes, which took the monkeys five days. What do I speak of a great archer like Lord Rama; even an amateur like me could have done that job.'

Unable to tolerate the ridicule of his master, Hanuman challenged Arjuna. 'Why speak of the entire monkey army, no flimsy bridge of arrows can handle the weight of an old monkey like me.'

This kind of confidence on the part of a mere monkey kindled the warrior-spirit of Arjuna. He took up the challenge with full gusto. He declared that if the bridge of arrows he constructs across the lake succumbs to the weight of the old monkey, then he would enter the fire and end his life. The monkey readily accepted the challenge. Arjuna readied himself to accomplish his newfound mission. Stringing an arrow to his bow, Arjuna intensely chanted mantras. Invoking higher powers, he released his arrow that sped across the lake and multiplied itself into billions of shafts that neatly intertwined, forming a sturdy bridge from one side of the lake to the other.

With a proud flick of his hand, Arjuna invited the old monkey to step onto his wonder creation. The monkey smartly walked up to the bridge and instead of stepping on it, turned around and faced Arjuna. Gently, he lowered his tail on the bridge. As soon as the tail touched the bridge of arrows, all the arrows disintegrated. Arjuna was aghast!

The old monkey spoke, 'Perhaps you have not done your best. Probably, you calculated my weight wrong. I will give you another chance. Go ahead and make another attempt.'

Arjuna was flustered at this offer. Anyway, he decided to take it up. This time though, he was much more focused and took the task very seriously. It wasn't as easy as he thought it was. He built a triple-layered bridge of arrows. The lower layers were sturdier than the upper ones. Once ready, he approached the monkey, this time, with hesitation. Like before, the monkey merely placed his tail in the beginning. The bridge stood! He then climbed the bridge. As he reached the middle of the bridge, he pushed it a bit with his weight. The entire bridge gave way and he fell into the lake. He swam out with a grin on his face.

Arjuna was disgusted with himself. He felt that he had no right to live now as a disgraced kshatriya. He lit a huge fire and was preparing to throw himself into it when he felt a tap on his shoulders. He turned behind to find a brilliantly-shining brahmin, who said, 'I understand you have lost a challenge and, therefore, you are preparing to enter into this fire. But, no challenge is considered complete without a witness. Did you appoint a witness to neutrally observe and take a decision?'

Both Arjuna and the old monkey shook their heads and accepted their mistake. The intelligent brahmin urged them to repeat the task again, this time, with him as the witness. Arjuna was delighted to have another opportunity. He prepared himself and this time rather than relying on his strength and abilities, he decided to rely on his worshipable master Krishna. He prayed to Krishna silently and fervently for empowerment to accomplish what seemed an impossible task. He had definitely been humbled, but now his life was at stake. After sufficiently supplicating, Arjuna raised his Gandiva bow and shot an array of arrows building an extremely sturdy bridge that according to him could accommodate an entire army.

The brahmin urged the monkey to climb on it. Arjuna watched with his heart in his mouth as the monkey steadily walked up. Reaching the middle of the bridge, the monkey began to shake the bridge with all his might. The bridge held firm. The monkey then began to jump up and down on the bridge, smashing it with all his strength. The bridge held firm. The old monkey expanded himself and assumed a huge form, manifesting himself as Hanuman. The form of Hanuman was so huge that Arjuna appeared like an ant in comparison. Still, the bridge held firm!

This time, both Arjuna and Hanuman were bewildered at what was happening. Hanuman quickly returned to his regular form and stepped out of the bridge. That's when both of them realised that the brahmin who was to bear witness was missing. They looked around and finally found him coming out of the waters of the lake.

He was bleeding all over his shoulders and neck. When the two great heroes saw him they realised what had transpired. They ran up to the brahmin and fell at his feet. Each of them caught one of his feet and began to cry. The brahmin assumed his original form as Lord Krishna. Picking up both his ardent devotees, he embraced them. After begging forgiveness a million times, Arjuna and Hanuman felt a bit relieved for their gross mistake of allowing their worshipable Lord to go through such a trauma of holding up the entire bridge of arrows on his shoulders, painfully bearing the mountainous weight of Hanuman.

Arjuna vowed never to underestimate and comment on anybody's strength. Hanuman vowed never to interfere and unnecessarily test any devotee of the Lord. Under the direction of Lord Krishna, Hanuman promised to be present on the flag of Arjuna and assist in the war against the Kauravas.

The intelligent make a complete fool of themselves when they underestimate the intelligence of those who appear like complete fools.

A Power-packed Meeting

He couldn't believe what he was seeing. She was shining like the sun today. Gorgeous was an understatement to describe her beauty. His pace increased as he began to approach his wife excitedly. His eyes were riveted on her effulgent face. She was seated on the riverbank, looking quizzically at something. Though he couldn't see her completely from the vantage point he was at, he realised she was holding on to something she considered extremely precious.

Bhima gasped at the sight that greeted him when he stood right next to her. A thousand-petalled golden lotus was in the hands of Draupadi. Whoever had seen a golden lotus and, that too, a thousand-petalled one? No wonder Draupadi was so transfixed with it. The flower was so radiant that its effulgence reflected on Draupadi's face.

Observing her husband stare at the unique flower, Draupadi explained, 'This flower came floating down the river. Its heavenly smell attracted me. Even from a few yojana, I could smell it. I was fortunate to reach this spot when it came bouncing down the river. I am sure there are more such flowers somewhere further along the river. Could you get more for me? Please.'

Her plea struck a chord in Bhima's heart. He realised that Draupadi had never asked him for anything until now. He had to fulfil this wish of his wife. He adored her and always wanted to do something for her and here was his chance. He set out immediately, following the course of the river. He was so happy! An enthusiastic Bhima began to blow the conch shell, heralding to the world that he was on a mission to please his wife. The blaring sound sent all the animals reeling in pain. Their eardrums were splitting and they all began to run helter-skelter in fear.

Suddenly, a deafening noise was heard and the ground below Bhima's legs began to quake. He froze! He looked around to ascertain what was happening. It happened again with more intensity. To Bhima, it appeared that someone was hitting the ground so hard that the entire tectonic plate was quaking and a tremor was being artificially generated under that impact. Bhima began to move towards the origin of the vibration. As he edged forward, the phenomenon continued a few more times and, now, only more vigorously.

'Oops!' Bhima unexpectedly almost tripped over something on his path. Regaining his balance, he looked below to find what was on his path. He was surprised to find what looked like a long tail. His eyes followed the path of the tail and found a huge elderly monkey resting on the ground. The monkey looked tired. Bhima was visibly irritated at this sight. How could a mere monkey dare to block the path of the mighty Bhima? Angrily, he ordered the old monkey to remove his tail from the path or else face dire consequences. The monkey seemed least bothered. He didn't even look towards Bhima. He spoke with his eyes closed and resting sideways on his elbows said, 'I am too old and exhausted to move now. If you like, you can move my tail yourself or even jump over it and proceed.'

Bhima was not happy with the answer. He said, 'O old monkey, it's not right etiquette to step over an elderly person. Not just that, I know for a fact that God resides within everyone's heart and stepping over anyone is akin to stepping over God. If that were not the case, I would have surely jumped over you as easily as my hero, Hanuman, had crossed the 100-yojana ocean.'

Hearing Hanuman's name, the monkey spoke, 'Who is this Hanuman that you respect so much?' Bhima was utterly surprised to know that this monkey didn't know about Hanuman, one of his own people. 'You seem to be a lazy monkey, unaware of anything in this world. Otherwise, how would you not know Hanuman, the son of the Wind God, the war hero of the Ramayana. He is, in fact, my brother. And, I have the same prowess as Hanuman.'

The monkey didn't seem impressed with Bhima's explanation. He only said, 'I am too old to even understand what strength is. If my tail is on your way, just do the needful and go your way.'

Bhima was frustrated with the monkey's attitude. He walked towards the tail and with two fingers, picked it up... It didn't budge! He then used his hand to pick up the tail. He couldn't move it even a wee bit. Flustered, he used both his hands. Nothing! Now, he put his entire might with both his hands and used his full body weight to pluck out the tail from the ground. Absolutely nothing! The tail seemed stuck to the ground. No matter how much he tried, he couldn't do anything at all. He heaved and cried. He was perspiring profusely. His eyes were rolling over. His mind was reeling. His ego was hurting.

How could this be? A person with the strength of 10,000 elephants unable to move an old monkey's tail! He gazed at the monkey. The old monkey was coolly smiling with his head raised, placed on his bent hand, watching the fun. Bhima walked up to the old monkey with folded hands and fell at his feet, humbly requesting him to reveal his real identity.

Instantly, the old monkey disappeared and in his place stood the powerful Hanuman in full glory. Bhima had tears of joy in his eyes. He was thrilled to see his heroic brother. Hanuman picked up Bhima and embraced him. Both the heroes exchanged notes on their lives and Hanuman taught Bhima important war tactics and martial art lessons. He promised Bhima that during the impending war, he would be seated on the flag of Arjuna. Keeping his word, during the war, whenever Bhima let out his war cries, Hanuman would join him and, together, their thunderous roars would strike terror in the hearts of the enemies, thereby diminishing their morale.

Before departing, Hanuman revealed to Bhima the source of the fragrant 'Saugandika' flowers that he had come to fetch for Draupadi. After finding those flowers easily, Bhima returned to a happy Draupadi. *

Arrogance is the weakness of the strong and simplicity is the strength of the weak.

---

* The place where this incident is believed to have happened is now famous as Hanuman Chati. It is situated close to Badrinath.

A Hairy Tale

'Where is Lord Rama today? Where is Hanuman today? Unless I see them I don't believe in their existence. Ask them to come in front of me and bear witness. If they don't come, then you all shall remain beggars forever.' King Kumaarpala walked away after speaking sternly to the brahmins of Kanyakubja.

The brahmins of Kanyakubja had been in possession of about 4,400 villages till now. They claimed that their ancestors were gifted these villages by Lord Rama, with Hanuman as the witness. But King Kumaarpala felt all this was humbug and made up. Education had given him the clarity to not believe in anything that he couldn't see or that didn't have tangible proof. He asked them to produce evidence before reclaiming their property.

Being stripped off all their possessions overnight, the brahmins had no option but to make an attempt to procure some proof. Three thousand of them proceeded on foot towards the southern direction in the hope that somehow, somewhere, they would meet Hanuman or Lord Rama. Traversing dense forests, steep mountains, crossing rivers, they ate fruits and roots only once a day. One day, they couldn't find anything to eat; they were running out of their supplies of water and food as well. Exhausted and fatigued, they could venture no further. Helplessly, they began to offer fervent prayers to Lord Rama.

Just then, an old ascetic approached them. He almost appeared from nowhere. Seeing the densely-populated entourage, he asked them the purpose of their travel. When he heard that they were travelling towards Rameshwaram to meet Hanuman and Lord Rama, the old ascetic heavily discouraged them and walked away. However, the brahmins decided not to lose hope but continue in their quest till the last breath. They now marched forward, sustaining only on their willpower.

The next day, another mysterious-looking ascetic met them and also discouraged their madness. He told them that he had been wandering all over the country and had never spotted Hanuman, Lord Rama, nor anything even remotely divine. He told them these were just fairy tales and not to be taken seriously. One of the brahmins got suspicious about this ascetic and asked, 'You have been discouraging us from yesterday. Are you Hanuman?'

The old ascetic smiled broadly. All the brahmins were shocked to see him transform into their worshipable master, Hanuman. Soon, 3000 brahmins were on their knees, taking shelter in the dynamic son of the Wind God. One particularly enthusiastic brahmin spoke up, 'O great hero, we have a request. In case you are pleased with our devotion, kindly show us your gigantic form that you assumed during the Ramayana War. We are all dying to see that avatar.'

Pleased with the sincerity of the brahmins, Hanuman obliged and showed them his gigantic form. Tears flowed freely from their eyes as they beheld the spectacular form of the Monkey God. Hanuman kneeled down and extended the huge palm of his right hand in front of them. It was filled with thousands of succulent fruits. He spoke to them in a thunderous voice, 'My dear brahmins, take these fruits and eat them. They will completely satisfy your hunger and will fill you with joy.'

Each brahmin picked up a fruit and ate it. They indeed felt very nourished and completely blissful. Now, Hanuman resumed his original form and stood amidst them. Abruptly, he did something that totally took them by surprise. He lifted his right arm and took out some hair from his armpit and put them inside a small-coloured pouch. He repeated the same process with his left armpit but he used a pouch of another colour this time. He wrapped both the pouches with tree bark and placed them under the care of one of the brahmins.

He then told them to hear his instructions very carefully. They had to return to Kanyakubja and instruct the King to return their lands and other possessions. If he failed to do so, they were to use the left pouch. And once the King repented and begged them to forgive him, they were to use the right pouch. If they followed his instructions carefully, the lands could be theirs soon. Hearing these inspiring and hope-giving words of Hanuman, the brahmins became joyful and began to dance. In fact, many of them went up to Hanuman's tail and began to kiss it. Hanuman was delighted seeing the joy on the faces of these innocent devotees.

Hanuman then walked up to a rocky mountain close by and broke a huge chunk of rock and flattened it. He then placed the flattened rock on the ground and asked all the 3000 brahmins to rest on it for the night. Reassuring them of his personal protection all night, Hanuman disappeared.

Following the advice of Hanuman, the brahmins mounted the rock and slept peacefully.

Whilst they were fast asleep, the rock was airlifted and gently carried towards Kanyakubja. Within five hours, the rock covered the distance they had taken months to traverse. As the gigantic rock began its descent in the province of Kanyakubja, hundreds gathered around to witness the miracle. When the brahmins woke up, they were surprised to find themselves amidst the villagers of Kanyakubja. When they realised what had happened, they all offered a prayer of gratitude to Hanuman for saving them so much trouble.

The happy brahmins straightway proceeded to the palace of the King to confront him. They narrated their experience about meeting Hanuman and requested the King to return their lands immediately if he didn't want to incur the wrath of the Monkey God. The King didn't pay any heed to their request since he hardly believed that they had actually met Hanuman. He wasn't going to believe in fairy tales. He was very clear.

Seeing the King's haughty demeanour and after receiving the signal from the other brahmin, the one who was carrying the pouches given to him by Hanuman, threw down the contents of the left pouch. The King only laughed, seeing hair falling from the pouch. As the shrill laughter of the King echoed in the courtroom, the brahmins left with a smile on their faces. They knew that their task was over and the King's choice was over; now, the Monkey God's role would begin.

As they left the palace, they saw smoke emitting from all directions. People began to run out of the palace. Soon, the entire palace was on fire. In a matter of minutes, every section of the palace was consumed by huge balls of fire.

Soon, the King came running out in great haste, his eyes filled with despair. He was a different man. There was humility written all over his face. His pride was burnt along with his palace. He fell at the feet of the brahmins with tears of repentance in his eyes. No words came from his mouth. There was nothing left to speak now.

Seeing the condition of the King, the kind brahmins opened the second right pouch and threw its contents. Instantly, the fire died and the palace was restored to its original splendour. One couldn't ever say there was such a huge fire a few moments ago. On entering his royal courtroom, the first thing that the King did was to issue an order to return the lands to the brahmins and he also passed a decree that the lands would belong to them forever. High above, Hanuman had a pleasant smile on his face, looking at the rejoicing brahmins.

Clouds of mercy hover over rain of tears.

Monkeys on a Rampage

'What! A saint who performs miracles! That's great! I have always heard of miracle-saints, but never met one. Get him to my court right away.' The Mughal King instructed his minister, who had informed him about a mystic saint who was becoming very famous in his kingdom. When the King heard that throngs of people, Hindus and Muslims alike, were visiting him to seek his blessings, he developed a desire to meet the saint. Of course, his intention was not to gain his blessings as much as it was to witness his miracles live.

Soon, the famous saint was at his court. Being a great devotee of Lord Rama, this saint was constantly immersed in uninterrupted chanting of the holy names of the Lord. 'Rama...Rama...Rama...' Even when he stood in front of the King, he continued chanting, unabated. He commanded such respect that as soon as he entered the royal court, every single person in the courtroom stood up in veneration with folded hands. Even the King was taken aback at the respect that he commanded and that people offered. Of course, the King wasn't a sentimentalist like the common men of his kingdom. He believed in logic first and in magic later. Interesting combination, he thought.

Without even offering his respects, nay any hospitality, the King arrogantly hurled an instruction at the saint. 'Do some miracle for my pleasure! I have heard of your mystic powers. I want to see a good demonstration now. Let me see how much of it is true.'

Saying this, he sat back and relaxed in his royal throne expecting some fantastic feat. The saint humbly folded his hands and said, 'My dear King, I am no magician. I have no mystic powers. The only miracle I know is to purify dirty hearts with the power of the holy names of Lord Rama.'

The saint had no desire for any cheap adoration by exhibiting his mystic powers. He clarified that mystic powers were gifts of God that should be discreetly used to bring people closer to God and serve humanity. They were not meant for garnering 'name and fame'. The saint's answer shocked the King. He glared at his minister in anger. How could anyone refuse the all-powerful monarch?

The King declared, 'Throw this pretender into the prison cell! He deserves nothing but flogging.'

On their King's command, the royal guards ran up to the saint and caught hold of his arms. The saint made no protest. He simply folded his hands, closed his eyes and began chanting the names of Lord Hanuman. He began chanting slowly, and within seconds, he started singing his prayers in a high-pitched voice. Everyone in the courtroom was stunned to silence.

Soon, glasses began to break in every corner of the courtroom; flower vases started shattering and screams could be heard from every nook of the palace. Within moments, hundreds and thousands of monkeys began to rush into the courtroom from all directions. They began to ravage everything they could lay their hands on. They tore down cushions from the seats in the courtroom; they pulled down all the upholsteries; they threw glasses and cups around, they broke all the weapons, snatching them from the scared soldiers; they did not even hesitate to tear the hair out of every soldier's and minister's beard. The courtroom was a total mess. Hundreds of monkeys kept pouring in. Soon, they dirtied every corner of the palace and destroyed every object they could grab.

The nuisance that the monkeys were causing maddened the King. He had no idea how to handle this catastrophe. Standing on his own throne to stay away from the monkeys, he trembled with fear. He noticed the saint, standing right in the middle of the chaos, completely composed. His eyes were closed and his lips were intensely chanting prayers. Surprisingly, none of the monkeys had touched him. In fact, a couple of monkeys were seated very peacefully near his feet, staring at him gracefully.

The King stepped down from his throne and ran up to the saint. Falling at his feet, he beseeched him to call off the monkey rampage and forgive him for his gross mistake. As the King repeatedly begged for forgiveness, the saint opened his eyes and stopped chanting. As soon as the saint stopped the incantations, all the monkeys walked away quietly. Soon, the courtroom was devoid of monkeys. But it was also devoid of its elegance and royalty. More than that, it had also been robbed of its pride and arrogance.

Yes, the King did witness a miracle that day. Yes, the saint did perform a miracle that day. A miracle that changed the King's heart forever!

Show magic is for temporary entertainment of the heart.
Real magic is for the permanent transformation of the heart.

Hanuman Temples

Jakhu Hanuman, Simla, Himachal Pradesh

Jakhu Temple is a famous Hanuman temple in Simla, the capital of Himachal Pradesh, a state in North India. The word 'Jakhu' is derived from the word 'Yaaku' or 'Yaksha'. The hill is the abode of gods like Yakshas, Kinnaras, Nagas and Asuras.

During the battle between Lord Rama and Ravana at Lanka, Lakshmana was injured by an arrow from Indrajit, Ravana's son, and rendered unconscious. To save his life, Hanuman flew towards the Himalayas to get the Sanjivani, a life-saving herb, which was only available on a specific mountain. All of a sudden, he saw a sage named Yaaku on Mount Jakhu. This place was named Jakhu after the same sage. In order to gather more details about the herb, Hanuman landed on this mountain. As a result of the power with which Hanuman landed on Mount Jakhu, the mountain which was earlier much taller, sank into the Earth, and was reduced to half its original size. After getting all the information about the herb, Hanuman resumed his journey towards Mount Drona, where the Sanjivani herb was available.

Hanuman had promised the sage Yaaku that he would meet him on his way back. However, due to shortage of time and as a result of an encounter with a demon named Kalanemi (whom he had killed after a tough fight), Hanuman had to rush to Lanka, using a shorter route. Since Hanuman did not come back, Sage Yaaku sage became very sad.

Just then, Hanuman expanded himself and a form of Hanuman appeared before the sage and told him the reason for his inability to keep his promise. After giving the sage an explanation, when Hanuman disappeared, Hanuman's deity manifested in the same place. This deity can be seen in the Jakhu Temple even today. This temple of Hanuman was constructed by Sage Yaaku sage in remembrance of the Monkey God.

Salasar Balaji, Churu, Rajasthan

This famous Hanuman temple is located in the Churu district of Rajasthan, in India. Since the name of the village where this is located is Salasar, the temple is famous as Salasar Balaji all over the country. The Hanuman deity here is regarded as very influential and has a beard and moustache. The temple was established in 1811 by Shri Mohan Dasji who was well-known amongst all as a great devotee of Hanuman. The deity was found from an agricultural field in the nearby village of Asota. The beautiful Balaji deity is seated on a golden throne here. There is a holy flame which keeps burning through the day and is believed to have been burning since the installation of the deity. Also, there has been a 24-hour narration of the Ramayana along with the chanting of Lord Rama's holy names for many years.

There are several famous stories based on interesting episodes and incidents related to Shri Mohan Dasji and Balaji. His samadhi (tomb) is located near the temple. Salasar Balaji is especially famous for removing ill-effects of black magic on small children. Lakhs of pilgrims visit this temple during the festival season throughout the year.

Hanuman Dhara, Chitrakoot, Madhya Pradesh

Hanuman Dhara is one of the most famous places of pilgrimage in Central India and is said to be the resting place of Hanuman. This is located at Chitrakoot, in Madhya Pradesh. The Hanuman Dhara Temple is situated inside a cave on a mountain peak. The deity is formed from natural rock and a natural stream of water falls on the tail of Hanuman. The story is that after the coronation of Lord Rama, Hanuman requested for a permanent place to settle down, where the injuries and burns on his tail could heal. Lord Rama shot an arrow and spurted a stream of water from the tip of the mountain, where he asked Hanuman to rest. Lord Rama told Hanuman that the stream of water would fall on his tail and relieve him of the burning sensation.

Bhadra Maruti, Khuldabad, Maharashtra

Bhadra Maruti Temple is located at Khuldabad, a small town in the Aurangabad district of Maharashtra. This temple is one of the two places where Hanuman is seen in a sleeping position. The other one is in Allahabad. The temple was built by Rajarishi Bhadrasen.

King Bhadrasen, a kind and pious man ruled Khuldabad, previously known by the name of Badravati Nagar. King Bhadrasen used to sing devotional songs in praise of Hanuman on the banks of Bhadrakund pond. One day, while the King was singing, Hanuman appeared in front of him. Listening to the captivating music, Hanuman fell asleep on the ground. Later, pleased by the great devotion of King Bhadrasen, Hanuman granted him a wish.

The King wished that Hanuman would stay there forever and fulfil the desires of all his devotees. Hanuman granted the wish and disappeared. After some time, a Hanuman deity in a sleeping posture was found, exactly where he had previously granted audience to the King. The name Bhadra Maruti or 'Sleeping Hanuman' was accorded to him after this incident. The Sleeping Hanuman deity is covered with an orange-coloured sheet and garlanded with a string of banyan leaves.

Kanapata Hanuman

This is the story of a historical tug-of-war, which took place between the demons and the demigods, in order to obtain the celestial nectar and be blessed with the boon of immortality. The tug-of-war happened in the middle of an ocean and the churning rod was Mount Mandara; the rope used for churning was a huge snake named, Vasuki. During this churning, many things appeared out of the ocean. One of the divine personalities that emerged from this churning was Lakshmi (Goddess of Wealth and Fortune). She was married to Lord Vishnu. Since Lakshmi emerged from the ocean, she was known as the daughter of the ocean. Thus, by marrying the daughter of the ocean, the Lord became the son-in-law of the ocean and the ocean became the father-in-law of Lord Vishnu—also known as Lord Jagannath—who is the presiding deity in Jagannath Puri.

During the night, the waves of the ocean would make a loud sound engulfing the city of Puri. Once, this sound entered Jagannath's temple, and disturbed the Lord's sleep. Lord Jagannath ordered Samudra not to make any sound, which might disturb Him. From then on, the sound of Samudra crashing on the beach never entered Jagannath's temple. Moreover, Lord Jagannath had deputed his devotee, Hanuman, to keep guard at the south gate and listen attentively, ensuring that the sound never entered the temple. Kanapata means to engage the ears ('kana' in Sanskrit) for hearing. Thus, Hanuman is known as Kanapata Hanuman in this region.

Vargi Hanuman

The Vargi Hanuman Temple is situated on Lokanatha Road, towards the west of Jagannath Temple in Jagannath Puri. Formerly, the Vargis (a clan from Maharashtra) would pass this way on their horses and disturb the peaceful temple environment, creating a nuisance for the people of Puri. These Vargis were devotees of Hanuman, and so to stop them from entering Puri, a Hanuman deity was installed in this area. Being loyal devotees of Hanuman, the Vargis did not dare to make any noise in front of this temple from that day on. As a result, the serenity and purity of the temple of Jagannath Puri was restored by Hanuman's presence. This is why Hanuman is called Vargi Hanuman in this part of the world.

Bedi Hanuman

The Bedi Hanuman is a small temple situated towards east of the Jagannath Temple in Puri. When the Jagannath Temple was built, Varuna (the Ocean God), wanted to enter the temple and pay his respects to Jagannath. However, whenever he would try to do so, the waves of the ocean would damage the temple structures. In order to protect the architecture of the temple and maintain its cleanliness, Lord Vishnu had the temple moved to a more interior part of Puri, so that the ocean would be far away from the temple. During the same time, a small temple for Hanuman was built nearby and Hanuman was asked to stay here and guard the Jagannath Temple from any damage caused by the ocean waves. Once, when the Ocean God tried to enter the temple, Hanuman used his mace to shoo him off.

The people of Orissa (now Odisha) being economically poor, could offer only a simple meal comprising rice and dal (split beans) to Hanuman. The Monkey God started missing the fine cuisine of Ayodhya. So, he relinquished his post and went back to Ayodhya to treat himself to some long-missed delicacies.

Using his absence as an excuse, the Ocean God decided to enter the Jagannath Temple. Lord Vishnu had to intervene and he moved the temple further inland. Finally, Lord Vishnu met Hanuman and scolded him for abandoning his duties. Hanuman was repentant and went back to the service of guarding the temple from the ocean waves. However, he could forget neither his hunger pangs nor the cuisine of Ayodhya. He kept abandoning his post and the ocean waves kept entering the temple, causing much damage to the structure. Lord Vishnu had to constantly move the temple further inland. This continued for some time.

Eventually, Lord Vishnu got really upset and bound Hanuman using chains ('bedi' in Sanskrit), so that he could not escape again. As a result, Hanuman is still (seen) standing, chained to a post near the ocean, keeping guard over the Jagannath Temple of Puri.

Tapasvi Hanuman

This Hanuman deity is located at the north gate of Jagannath Temple as a protector of the temple. He is also known as Chari-chakra Hanuman and Ashta-bhuja Hanuman. Chari-chakra means he is holding four chakras (discs) in his hands and ashta-bhuja means he has eight hands. This Hanuman deity is four-feet in height and faces the eastern direction.

Once the Sudarshan Chakra, the powerful celestial disc of the Lord became very proud and thought, 'I am so close to Lord Jagannath and most dear to him.' Lord Jagannath is famous for destroying pride, and did not like Sudarshan Chakra's arrogance. The Sudarshan Chakra thought he was most powerful as the Lord is protected by him and dependent upon him; the Lord takes his help to accomplish any difficult job. Thus, the Lord decided to teach him a lesson for his own good.

The Lord sent the Sudarshan Chakra to call for Hanuman. At that time, Hanuman was engrossed in meditation. Immediately, the Sudarshan Chakra went to inform Hanuman that Lord Jagannath wanted to see him, and Hanuman started his journey to meet his Lord. After informing Hanuman, the Sudarshan Chakra immediately returned to the temple, reaching there before Hanuman did. As Hanuman neared the temple gates, the Sudarshan Chakra started to move very fast around the temple premises, blocking Hanuman's path, preventing him from reaching the Lord.

Hanuman thought, "How can I meet my Lord?" He took shelter in Lord Jagannath by chanting his holy names. Instantly, by the mercy of the Lord, Hanuman was empowered and he developed six extra arms from his shoulders. Thus, he became the ashta-bhuja Hanuman. Four hands held a Sudarshan Chakra (each): two hands were joined together offering respects, and the other two hands held the beads for chanting the holy names of the Lord.

Hanuman proceeded towards the inner sanctum to meet Lord Jagannath. After some time, the Sudarshan Chakra also reached there in great distress. Lord Jagannath wanted to punish the Sudarshan Chakra for offending Hanuman, and also wanted to destroy his great pride. The Sudarshan Chakra was ashamed to see that Hanuman was more powerful than him and he had not been able to prevent Hanuman from entering the temple. Thus, the Lord cursed the Sudarshan Chakra that in the Kali Yuga (Age of Kali), he would not have his discus form, rather, he would take the form of a pillar, which would always be to the left of Lord Jagannath.

The Sudarshan Chakra felt this to be too heavy a curse, and requested the Lord to reduce its severity. The most merciful Lord said, 'Do not fear. In the Kali Yuga, you will be situated at the top of my temple. When people see the Chakra, they will feel the same devotion as they would on seeing me.'

Since then, Tapasvi Hanuman has stood at the North Gate of the temple in Jagannath Puri, and the Sudarshan Chakra is situated atop the Jagannath Temple.

Chakrayapet Gandi Anjaneya, Cuddapah, Andhra Pradesh

This Hanuman temple is located in the Cuddapah district of Andhra Pradesh.

After killing Ravana, Lord Rama and Mother Sita along with Lakshmana, Hanuman and others were on their way to Ayodhya. According to legend, Hanuman would go ahead and search for a good place for all of them to stop by and rest on their journey back home.

Once Hanuman chose a cave by the side of a river, he marked the spot by hanging a golden rope across two hilltops so that the rope could be seen from a distance. The party did indeed stop by at the cave. Grateful for Hanuman's efforts, Lord Rama carved a picture of Hanuman on the stone walls of the cave.

In the early 1800s, Sir Thomas Munroe was the Collector of Cuddapah. Some people claim that, once, while travelling through the hills, he saw a shiny rope—seemingly made of gold—stretched across from one hill to another. When he mentioned this to others accompanying him, they were surprised as no one else could see the rope that Sir Thomas was referring to. Finally, an elderly man spoke, 'Anyone who can see the golden rope is blessed. But, he will die in a few months.' Sir Thomas looked at his companions in disbelief. In a few months, Sir Thomas died. It is believed that he even wrote about this incident in his diary.

A small temple stands at this place today. There is a carving of Hanuman on the stone walls, parts of which are covered in silver. This place bears testimony as a memorial to the great service offered by the loyal Hanuman to his master Lord Rama. There are pictures of Lord Rama and Mother Sita, including a picture of Sir Thomas Munroe that continues to surprise many pilgrims even today.

Ranamandala Anjaneya Swamy, Adoni, Andhra Pradesh

Adoni is well connected by rail and road. Guntakal, one of the biggest railway junctions, is a one-hour journey from Adoni. It is in the Kurnool district of Andhra Pradesh.

Lord Rama is believed to have visited this place during his exile. 'Rana' means war and 'mandala' means zone. So, Ranamandala means war zone. This was the place where Hanuman fought against demonic forces and destroyed them because they were a cause of disturbance for Lord Rama and Mother Sita. Hence, this place came to be known as Ranamandala.

Anjaneya Swamy, the Hanuman deity, is carved out of a monolithic rock on the top of Ranamandala Hills. The beautiful deity is smeared with Kesari (orange) colour. Legend has it that since the temple had to be built within a day, unlike other temples, this deity does not have a roof over it. Some believe it to be self-manifested while others consider it to have been consecrated by Vyasa Tirtha during his visit to this place.

Sri Mangarayaru Temple, Kurnool District, Andhra Pradesh

The famous pilgrim centre, Mantralayam, is in the Kurnool district of Andhra Pradesh.

Devotees and worshippers have to climb about 500 steps to reach the top of the hill. On the way up—amidst a panoramic view—there is a temple of Hanuman known as Santhana Anjaneya Swamy (bestower of progeny). The beautiful Lake Ramjal, at the foothills, is believed to have been present since time immemorial.

Below the hill, there is a shrine of Hanuman known as Mangarayaru Gudi (temple). Here stands one of the earliest idols of Hanuman consecrated by Vyasa Tirtha. The temple is under the auspices of Mantralaya Sri Raghavendra Swamy Mattha.

Panchamukha Hanuman, Kurnool, Andhra Pradesh

Sri Panchamukha Anjaneya was the main deity of Sri Raghavendra Swami—a great saint of the 16th century. This is the place where Sri Raghavendra Swami meditated on the five-faced form of Hanuman. It is now known as Panchamukhi, where a temple has been built for him. It is located on the south bank of River Tungabhadra near Manchala, now known as Mantralayam which is in the Kurnool district of Andhra Pradesh.

Hanuman assumed this form to kill Mahiravana, a powerful demoniac black magician, during the Ramayana War. Mahiravana had taken Lord Rama and Lakshmana as captives, and the only way to kill him was to extinguish five burning lamps—strategically positioned in different directions—all at the same time. Hanuman assumed his Panchamukha form and accomplished the task, thus killing the rakshasa, and freeing Lord Rama and Lakshmana.

This form of Hanuman is very popular, and is also known as Panchamukha (the one with five mouths) Anjaneya or Panchamukhi Anjaneya.

Yantroddharaka Hanuman, Hampi, Karnataka

One of the most beautiful and popular places in India is the birthplace of Hanuman—Hampi—which is located in the Hospet district of Karnataka. There are many hills in this area. One of the hills is called the Anjanadri Parvat. This is the mountain on which Hanuman was born. All the hills surrounding the Anjanadri Parvat were playgrounds of Hanuman and his friends. Their favourite sport included playing with huge boulders. They would make stacks of boulders and rocks, and keep them at various places on the mountains. In fact, if one visits Hampi today, one can find unique stone structures. The smaller stones are at the bottom and the bigger stones are balanced on them while they stand at the cliffs' edges, almost challenging the law of gravity.

In fact, Hanuman had met Lord Rama for the first time in a place called Malyavana Hill, which is not far from the Anjanadri Parvat in Hampi. In memory of this meeting, there is a temple of Lord Rama here, called Kodanda Rama Temple. Situated right behind the Kodanda Rama Temple, is a unique temple of Hanuman known as the Yantroddharaka Hanuman Temple.

There is an interesting story behind the origin of the Hanuman deity in this temple. A mystical story that amazes people each time they hear it. Vyasa Tirtha—born in 1460 AD in Mysore District, Karnataka, India—was a great scholar and a saint. The story dates back to the reign of King Krishna Deva Raya. Vyasa Tirtha used to go to a calm spot on the banks of River Tungabhadra and meditate for long hours. One day, while he was meditating, an image of Hanuman kept coming to his mind. Since this image continued flashing through his mind, he considered changing his location to see if the image appeared even then. To his surprise, he could not see any image of Hanuman if he sat anywhere else. It was only when he sat at that particular spot that he could see the image in his mind's eye.

Later that night, when he was asleep, Madhvacharya (another saintly person from Karnataka, India, and also believed to be an incarnation of Hanuman) appeared in the dreams of Vyasa Tirtha and instructed him to install the Anjaneya (Hanuman) diety. After this dream, Vyasa tirtha again went to the spot where he had previously seen the image of Hanuman, while meditating. He again sat at that very spot and began to meditate. Yet again, he saw the image of Hanuman appear in his mind's eye. Without any delay, he outlined that image on a nearby rock, using an angara (coal) as his pen. As soon as he finished drawing the image of Hanuman, to his astonishment, a monkey came to life from the drawing on the rock. The monkey jumped out of the rock and the drawing disappeared immediately. Vyasa Tirtha was pleasantly surprised and he repeated the process of drawing. Each time, a monkey would jump out of the rock and the drawing would disappear. This happened 12 times and a monkey emerged from the rock every single time. Thus, there were 12 monkeys around Vyasa Tirtha.

Amazed, Vyasa Tirtha finally decided to bind the image of Hanuman in a yantra (device; amulet). He first drew a yantra that looked like a six-cornered star. In the middle of the yantra, he drew the image of Hanuman sitting in padmasana (lotus position). The star was enclosed in a circle. And the circle that enclosed the star had flames going outwards, thus giving it the look of the sun. In order to make sure that Hanuman does not escape from the yantra, he made those 12 monkeys, which had previously emerged from the rock guard this yantra. He made the 12 monkeys stand in such a way that one monkey would hold the tail of the next, thus forming a closed benzene-like ring, which formed the outermost structure of the yantra. A careful look at the amulet revealed that the 12 monkeys stood like the hour-markers in a clock dial.

This is probably the only temple where Hanuman is seen in a seated posture. Generally, Hanuman deities are seen in standing, blessing or flying positions. Following this, it is believed that Vyasa Tirtha installed 732 Hanuman temples all over South India.

Namakkal Hanuman, Namakkal District, Tamil Nadu

This 18-foot tall Hanuman deity is located in the Namakkal district of Tamil Nadu, India.

After Hanuman placed the mountain of Sanjivini herb back in the Himalayas, on his journey back, he took a bath in the holy Gandaki River. There, he found a precious Salagrama (holy deity in the form of a round stone) of Lord Narasimha and Lord Ranganatha carved together in one. He decided to take it back with him for worship.

On his way, Hanuman stopped at a place for his evening prayers. The sacred Salagrama could not be placed on the ground. So, Hanuman looked for someone to hold it and found Goddess Mahalakshmi nearby. She agreed to hold it on one condition: if Hanuman got late, she would place the Salagrama on the ground. Hanuman got absorbed in meditation and failed to return on time. Mahalakshmi placed the Salagrama on the ground and the stone immediately transformed into a hill. On his return, the powerful Hanuman used his entire strength but could not move the hill even by an inch. Then, he heard a celestial voice, 'Hanuman, you are fortunate for having seen the special Salagrama. The Lord wants to give audience to Lakshmi and wants to reside here. The Lord is pleased with you and wants you to later come and stay here, serve him and protect his devotees.'

Hanuman became joyful when he heard this and prayed to Narasimha Deva and Lakshmi Devi before he returned. With the Lord's blessings, Hanuman killed the wicked demon and black magician Mahiravana. He helped to win the battle against Ravana and then returned to Ayodhya with Lord Rama.

Devotees believe that after Lord Rama returned to his abode, Hanuman came back to this place to serve Lord Narasimha. As Narasimha Deva stayed right at the centre of the Salagrama Hill, Hanuman could not see the Lord simply by standing at the level of the ground. So, Hanuman had to grow in size in order to see the divine feet of the Lord. Hanuman's eyes and Lord Narasimha Deva's foot are in a straight line and at the same height.

Hanuman Prayers

A prayer, according to its usual definition, is a solemn request for help or an expression of gratitude to God or a higher power of worship. But, when we understand the meaning of prayer in its true sense, we realise we pray out of fear, duty and love. Except for love, all other forms of prayers are motivated by some other (selfish) reason.

All of us in this world seek a perfect relationship—a relationship which never falls apart, one that assures perfect loyalty, which gives us a feeling of being protected and that which is not superficial. This need for shelter is supremely important and is a fundamental need of every human being.

A prayer can be defined as a form of communication between two beings—one is a shelter-giver and the other is the receiver. Praying is the act of seeing the invisible and entering the land of the unknown. Through prayer, the invisible becomes a beautiful vision, not only for our eyes, but our whole being. The heart becomes the window to that vision. The unknown land becomes familiar to us, even more than our very home. However, the biggest impediment in offering a heartfelt prayer, is the ego within. This is because praying is considered a sign of weakness. Accepting our weakness is also, in fact, an act of courage, for it gives us access to higher powers.

In this context, the story of the two ants serves as an important example. One ant challenged the other to jump from one hill to another. The second ant silently accepted the challenge. Then, it promptly climbed on the feet of a lion, which was about to pounce. The lion instantly jumped and easily landed on the next mountaintop. The recognition of our limitation allows us to accept help and shelter. This is when we can truly achieve the impossible. This story seems relevant and important as far as the ant is concerned. But, can we imagine a powerful personality like Hanuman doing the same thing? Taking shelter in someone else to achieve his goals? For a competent person to accept shelter is tough for the ego and that's exactly what Hanuman's life teaches us. His life is a rare combination of immense self-confidence and deep humility—both derived from his shelter in Lord Rama.

In fact, this combination does not show his lack of strength; on the contrary, it represents his unlimited strength of the heart. Just as a tree full of fruits is bent, a person who is filled with virtues is ready to bend and take shelter in the Lord with prayers.

This section comprises the chosen prayers which Hanuman offered to Lord Rama and also includes some prayers about the Monkey God himself. These prayers will help you make the right decisions; find the right direction and the desired destination on the road of life.

Narada Muni Praises Hanuman

From Sri Brhad Bhagvatamruta

(By Sri Sanatana Gosvami)

BB 1.4.64

sri narada uvaacha

satyam eva bhagvat-kripa-bharasyaaspadam

nirupamam bhavaan param

yo hi nityam ahaho mahaa-prabhosh

citra-citra-bhajanaamrtaarnavah

Sri Narada said: Hanuman, you are the greatest

recipient of the mercy of the Supreme Lord. You are

incomparable.

Ah! You are always immersed in

an ocean of ecstatic worship of the Lord, enjoying it

as newer and newer at every moment.

BB 1.4.65

daasah sakhaa vaahanam aasanam dhvajacchatram

vitaanam vyajanam ca vandi

mantri bhinag yodha-patih sahaayashrestoh

mahaa-kirti-vivardhanash ca

You are the Lord's servant, His friend, His carrier, His

seat, His flag, His umbrella, His canopy, His fan. You

are His bard, His adviser, His doctor, His general, His best helper, the expander of His infinite glories.

BB 1.4.66

samarpitaatmaa parama-prasaada-bhrut
tadeya-sat-kirti-kathaika-jivanah
tad-aashritaananda-vivardhanah sadaa
mahat-tamah shri-garudaadito dhikah

Having surrendered yourself entirely to the Lord, having received His highest mercy, having dedicated your life to topics of His transcendental glories, you always increase the bliss of the devotees sheltered by Him. You are the best of saints, greater even than others like Garuda.

BB 1.4.67

aho bhavaan eva vishuddha-bhaktimaan
param na sevaa-sukhato dhimanya yah
imam prabhuam vaacam udaara-shekharam
jagaada tad-bhakta-gaea-pramodinim

Indeed, your devotion for the Lord is absolutely pure, for you consider nothing more valuable than the pleasure of serving Him. You delighted all His

devotees by speaking to the best of generous Lords
these words:

BB 1.4.68

bhava-bandha-cchide tasyai

spruhayaami na muktaye

bhavaan prabhur aham daasa

iti yatra vilupyate

Even though liberation destroys the bondage of
material existence, I have no desire for liberation, in
which I would forget that You are the master and I
am Your servant.

Prayers to Hanuman

(Doha)

shri guru charan saroja-raj

nija manu mukura sudhaari

baranau raghubara bimala yasha

jo dayaka phala chari

budhee-heen tanu jannikay

sumirow pavana kumara

bala-budhee vidya dehoo mohe

harahu kalesha vikaara

Cleansing the mirror of my mind with the dust of the lotus-feet of the spiritual master, I describe the impeccable glory of Lord Rama, which bestows the four fruits of Righteousness (Dharma), Wealth (Artha), Pleasure (Kama) and Liberation (Moksha)

Considering myself as less intelligent, I remember Lord Hanuman. Praying earnestly to give me strength, intelligence and knowledge, while curing my body of all ailments and mind of mental imperfections.

(Chaupai)

jai hanuman gyan gun saagar

jai kapis tihun lok ujaagar...(1)

ram doot atulit bal dhaama

anjani putra pavan sut naama...(2)

Victory to Hanuman, ocean of knowledge and virtue,

Glory to Monkey Lord, illuminator of the three worlds...(1)

Lord Rama's envoy, abode of matchless power,

Anjana's son, named 'Son of the Wind'...(2)

mahavir vikram bajrangi

kumati nivar sumati ke sangi...(3)

kanchan varan viraj subesa

kanan kundal kunchit kesa...(4)

Mighty hero, strong as a thunderbolt,

Dispeller of evil thoughts and companion to the good...(3)

Golden-hued and splendidly clad,

Adorned with earrings and long curly locks...(4)

hath vajra aur dhwaja viraje

kaandhe moonj janeu saaje...(5)

shankar suvan kesri nandan

tej prataap maha jag vandan...(6)

In your hands shine divine mace and victory banner,

A sacred thread adorns your shoulder...(5)

Lord Shiva's son and Kesari's joy,

Your glory is revered throughout the world...(6)

vidyavaan guni ati chatur

ram kaj karibe ko aatur…(7)

prabhu charitra sunibe ko rasiya

ram Lakhan sita mann basiyaa…(8)

Supremely learned, virtuous and wise,

Ever intent on Lord Rama's service…(7)

You delight in hearing the Lord's deeds,

Lord Rama, Lakshmana, Mother Sita

dwell in your heart…(8)

sukshma roop dhari siyahi dikhava

vikat roop dhari lank jalava…(9)

bhim roop dhari asur sanhare

ramachandra ke kaj sanvare…(10)

In a tiny form you appeared before Sita,

Yet you burnt Lanka assuming a gigantic form…(9)

Taking a dreadful form you slaughtered demons,

And completed Lord Rama's mission…(10)

laye sanjivan lakhan jiyaye

shri raghuvir harashi ur laye…(11)

raghupati kinhi bahut badai

tum mama priya bharat-hi-sam bhai…(12)

Bringing the magic herb Sanjivani, you revived Lakshmana
And Lord Rama embraced you with delight...(11)
Greatly did Lord Raghu praise you,
"You are as dear to Me as My brother, Bharata"...(12)

sahas badan tumharo yash gaave
as kahi shripati kanth lagaave...(13)
sankadhik brahmaadi muneesa
narad sarad sahit aheesa...(14)

"May the thousand-mouthed Seshnaga sing your glory",
So saying Lord Rama, gave you an embrace...(13)
Sanak and the great sages, Lord Brahma, and the holy saints,
Along with Narada, Sarasvati and the King of Serpents...(14)

yam kuber dikpaal jahan te
kavi kovid kahi sake kahan te...(15)
tum upkar sugreevahin keenha
ram milaye rajpad deenha...(16)

Yama, Kuvera and the guardians of the quadrants,
Poets and scholars—none can truly express your glory...(15)
You rendered great service to Sugriva,
Bringing him to Lord Rama—you gave him kingship...(16)

tumhro mantra vibheeshana maana

lankeshwar bhaye sab jag jana...(17)

yug sahastra yojana par bhanu

leelyo tahi madhur phal janu...(18)

Vibhishana heeded your counsel,

And became Lanka's King, all the world knows...(17)

Though the sun is thousands of miles away,

You dashed at it, thinking it a delicious fruit...(18)

prabhu mudrika meli mukh mahee

jaladhi langhi gaye achraj nahee...(19)

durgam kaj jagat ke jete

sugam anugraha tumhre tete...(20)

Carrying the Lord's ring in your mouth,

You leapt across the Ocean—no wonder...(19)

All arduous tasks in this world,

Become easy, by your grace...(20)

ram duwaare tum rakhvare

hot na agya binu paisare...(21)

sab sukh lahai tumhari sarna

tum rakshak kahu ko darna...(22)

You guard Lord Rama's gate,

None enters without your consent...(21)

Your shelter rewards one joy
One under your protection should fear, why?...(22)

aapan tej samharo aapai
teenon lok hank te kanpai...(23)
bhoot pisaach nikat nahin aavai
mahavir jab naam sunavai...(24)
You alone can withstand your splendour,
The three worlds tremble when you roar...(23)
Ghosts and demons dare not come near,
When one utters your name—Mahavir...(24)

nase rog harae sab peera
japat nirantar hanumat beera...(25)
sankat se hanuman chhudavai
man kram vachan dhyan jo lavai...(26)
All disease and pain disappear,
Hanuman's name when people constantly chant and
hear...(25)
Hanuman frees one from all calamity
Who remember him in thought, word and activity...(26)

sab par ram tapasvee raja
tin ke kaj sakal tum saja...(27)

aur manorath jo koi lavai

soi amit jeevan phal pavai...(28)

Rama, the Lord of yoga reigns over all,

And you carry out His every task...(27)

Whoever yearns for you will undoubtedly be,

Sipping nectar through life contently...(28)

charon jug partap tumhara

hai parsiddh jagat ujiyara...(29)

sadhu sant ke tum rakhware

asur nikandan ram dulare...(30)

Your glory shines in four ages,

And fame radiates across the universe...(29)

You are the guardian of saints and sages,

Destroyer of demons and beloved of Lord Rama...(30)

ashta siddhi nav nidhi ke data

as var deen janki mata...(31)

ram rasayan tumhare pasa

sada raho raghupati ke dasa...(32)

You of eight siddhis, nine nidhis giver be,

As Mother Janaki gave this boon happily...(31)

You are the storehouse of Lord Rama's love, surely,

Remaining Lord Rama's servant ever unceasingly...(32)

tumhare bhajan ram ko pavai

janam janam ke dukh bisraavai...(33)

antkaal raghuvar pur jayee

jahan janam hari bhakt kahayee...(34)

Singing your praise, one finds Lord Rama,

Destroying the sorrows of countless lives past...(33)

At death, one goes to Lord Rama's own abode,

Ever to be known as His own...(34)

aur devta chitt na dharahin

hanumat sei sarv sukh karahin...(35)

sankat kate mite sab peera

jo sumirai hanumat balbeera...(36)

No need of any other deity,

Serving Hanuman, makes one happy...(35)

All affliction ceases, all pain disappears,

By remembering the mighty Hanuman...(36)

jai jai jai hanuman gosain

kripa karahun gurudev ki nayin...(37)

jo shat bar path kare koi

chhutahin bandi maha sukh hoi...(38)

Victory and glory to Lord Hanuman,

O Divine Guru, bless us with your grace...(37)

Whoever recites this a hundred times
Is released from all bondage and gains bliss...(38)

jo yeh padhe hanuman chalisa
hoye siddhi saakhi gaureesa...(39)
tulsidas sada hari chera
keejai nath hriday mahn dera...(40)

One reciting these prayers,
Achieves perfection, witness Lord Shiva bears...(39)
The Lord's ever servant Tulsidas requests,
"O Lord, may you always reside in my heart"...(40)

(Doha)
pavan tanay sankat harana
mangala murati roop
ram lakhana sita sahita
hriday basahu soor bhoop

O Son of Wind God, O Remover of Obstacles, O one
with an auspicious form. O King of Gods, kindly reside in
my heart with Lord Rama, Lakshmana and Sita.

Acknowledgements

Walking through life, I have always seen myself as a student, surrounded by teachers who have touched and enhanced my life immensely. I would like to express my heartfelt gratitude for all that I have been fortunate enough to learn from them.

To name all of them here would be impossible; however, two of the most prominent teachers in my life have been: H.D.G. A.C. Bhaktivedanta Swami Srila Prabhupada, the founder Acarya of the Hare Krishna Movement, and H.H. Radhanath Swami, the author of the international bestseller, *The Journey Home: Autobiography of an American Swami*.

I am grateful to my mentor, friend and well-wisher H.G. Govinda Prabhu who was the source of inspiration behind this book and every other book that I have written so far. His phenomenal wisdom and clarity have always enlightened me.

My special gratitude to Dr. Shrilekha Hada, who helped in the initial editing and proofreading of this book.

I would also like to thank Kanishka Gupta, profusely, for being the invisible hand that took this book to the world.

And of course, my warm thanks to the entire team of Om Books International, especially my publisher Ajay Mago, editor-in-chief Dipa Chaudhuri and my editor Ipshita Mitra—their sincere efforts and dedication are visible on every page of the book.